Twayne's Filmmakers Series

Warren French
EDITOR

David Lean

David Lean on location with Ryan's Daughter.

David Lean

MICHAEL A. ANDEREGG
University of North Dakota

BOSTON

Twayne Publishers

1984

David Lean

is first published in 1984 by Twayne Publishers
A Division of G. K. Hall & Company

Photographs on pages ii, 6 (bottom), 14, 24, 27, 36 (top), 59, 65, 77, 89, and 99 courtesy of *The Museum of Modern Art/Film Stills Archive*. Photographs on pages xx, 6 (top), 36 (bottom), 83 (bottom), and 104 courtesy of *Movie Star News*. Photographs on pages 83 (top), 98, 109, 120, 127, and 135 courtesy of *Cinemabilia*. Photographs on pages 22, 62, 80, and 124 courtesy of *Larry Edmunds Bookstore*.

Book Production by Marne B. Sultz

First Printing, October 1984

Printed on permanent/durable acid-free paper and
bound in the United States of America

Library of Congress Cataloging in Publication Data

Anderegg, Michael A.
David Lean.

(Twayne's filmmakers series)
Bibliography: p. 144
Filmography: p. 148
Includes index.
1. Lean, David, 1908- . I. Title. II. Series.
PN1998.A3L3792 1984 791.43′0233′0924 84-9003
ISBN 0-8057-9298-8

For Timothy

Contents

About the Author

MICHAEL A. ANDEREGG was born in Paris, France, in 1942. He was raised in Los Angeles, California, and attended UCLA, where he received the Bachelor of Arts degree in 1968. He received the Ph.D. in English literature from Yale University in 1972. He is the author of *William Wyler* (1979) in this series and of film-related articles for the *Michigan Quarterly Review, Film/Literature Quarterly,* and *North Dakota Quarterly.* He teaches English and film at the University of North Dakota and has been a visiting lecturer at Boston University.

Editor's Foreword

MICHAEL ANDEREGG has made an unusual contribution to this series of books primarily devoted to auteurist filmmakers, because his books have been studies of the thematic and stylistic similarities in the work of honored directors who have not been thought of primarily as auteurs. In the foreword to Anderegg's *William Wyler,* I asked what indeed Wyler was doing among a group of advocates and creators of "personal cinema," far removed from his own meticulous work, especially in the transformation of literary classics into memorable films at the height of the Hollywood "studio system" in the 1930s and 1940s. Briefly, the answer is that he created a uniquely excellent body of work that not only entitled him to the American Film Institute's fourth annual award of life achievement (1976), but also merited Anderegg's detailed analysis of the trademarks of films like *Jezebel, The Letter, Wuthering Heights,* and *The Best Years of Our Lives* that have become classics of the cinematic repertoire.

David Lean has done most of his work since the decline of the "studio system," which was breaking down in Great Britain even before its largely court-enforced demise in the United States; and his responsibility for several of the blockbusting epic films of the romantic 1960s has seen his name achieve a familiarity generally accorded only the most gifted auteurists. Yet, despite the efforts of partisans to establish his credentials as an auteur, one applies the label to him uneasily. As Michael Anderegg concludes, *Ryan's Daughter* (1970), Lean's last film to date, "demonstrates the limitations of the auteur theory, at least as it has been promulgated in this country." I am quite in agreement, for I feel that attempting to enshrine David Lean as an auteur overextends the term to the point where it loses the unique value that I believe it has for understanding one aspect of film as an art. The problem may be traced to enthusiasts who insist on treating auteurism as *the* key to understanding film history, rather than *a* key. Even Andrew Sarris, who is not guilty of this oversimplification, goes too far, I think, when he includes both William Wyler and David Lean among those whose work delivers "less than meets the eye." The note of condescension here arises from the unstated premise that films must necessarily include "more than meets the eye"—an intellectual position not entirely consistent with mastery in the visual arts.

To bolster my argument that David Lean is not usefully classified as an auteur, but needs to be respected as another kind of creator vitally important to the flourishing of film, I am going to draw evidence from a work that while not directed and produced by David Lean, stars him, records his personal convictions, and apparently has been endorsed by him as a "self-portrait."

In fact, *David Lean: A Self-Portrait*, produced and directed by Thomas Craven in 1971, just after the release of *Ryan's Daughter*, is one of the two most useful introductions to the work and psyche of a director in the valuable, but so far limited, documentary genre.

This tidily organized film is divided into three parts. The first is an introduction to Lean's films, although it includes only ten of the fifteen: two attempts at comedy, *Blithe Spirit* and *Hobson's Choice*, and three domestic dramas, *This Happy Breed*, *The Passionate Friends*, and *Madeleine*, are passed over in utter silence, leaving the suggestion that Lean's work has enjoyed greater commercial success and continuity of development than it has as a whole. The second part is Lean's lengthy acknowledgment of the importance to his films of the contributions of scriptwriters, actors, cinematographers, art directors, and set designers, emphasizing especially Lean's statement that "the script is the most important thing in the whole film." The third part, about half of the film's one-hour length, is devoted to expounding what might be called the "obligations" of a professional—the director's handling of crowd and sex scenes, financial responsibilities to his sponsors, his relationship to critics and the public, culminating in the statement that one choosing this "lonely job" has to be "a bit of a dreamer," yet also has "certainly got to be practical" (this last sentiment surely not shared by such conspicuous auteurs as D. W. Griffith, Erich von Stroheim, and Francis Ford Coppola).

It would be difficult to provide a better introduction to a distinguished director's conception of his job and his major accomplishments. To put this film into perspective, however, we need to contrast it with *Fellini: A Director's Notebook*, made by Federico Fellini for Italian television in 1969 and now available theatrically. Here we find no neat chronological catalog of Fellini's major films, no orderly citation of the contributions of others to his work, and certainly no moralizing review of the director's obligations to backers, critics, or viewers. Rather the disoriented audience is bombarded by a quick succession of seemingly random sequences commenting on the director's abandoned projects and work in progress, along with scenes cut from an early film and episodes dramatizing Fellini directing, entertaining, and interviewing a grotesque group of supplicants in his office. It is impossible to take the space here to point out the method in this madness; but it should be observed that all of the episodes are delightfully comic, yet undershot by the same melancholy that provides a continuing stream through Fellini's feature films.

A striking difference between the Lean and Fellini films is that the former is an elegantly phrased and illustrated lecture on the director's thoughts and achievements, whereas the latter is a bizarre series of visions that entertain the viewer, but from which he must draw his own conclusions, if any.

This difference takes us back to the starting point of the auteurist controversy in François Truffaut's articles "Une certaine tendance du cinéma français" in the January 1954 issue of *Cahiers du Cinéma.* Truffaut objected to the preeminence of the scriptwriter in filmmaking and the director's functioning as "the gentleman who adds the pictures." Against this procedure, Truffaut poses the prospect of "un cinéma d'auteurs" created by those who often write and invent what they film. As Annette Insdorf explains matters in her book on Truffaut in this series, "he is seeking the personal touch—the man behind or inside the work—the manifestation of a human sensibility molding an art form to communicate its obsessions." This last sentence surely describes *Fellini: A Director's Notebook* as well as the Italian's feature films. On the other hand, Lean's governing sentiment that the "script is the most important thing in the whole film" and his distrust of improvisation describe the traditional practice that Truffaut zealously protested. Even the terms "self-portrait" and "director's notebook," familiar from another visual art, suggest the difference between a finished, objective, distanced painting and the kind of spontaneous sketches that are now often the most highly prized works of some painters.

Most revealing of all is Lean's concluding avowal in *Self-Portrait*: "I don't feel that I'm capable of making great statements about life," surely the farthest austere remove from Truffaut's search for "a human sensibility molding an art form to communicate its obsessions." Lean fits precisely Truffaut's concept of a *metteur en scène;* but we must resist placing any pejorative connotation on this term and judge the individual within the framework of his aspirations.

Like William Wyler, David Lean has enjoyed his greatest success in transforming the literary works of others like Noel Coward and Charles Dickens into visual parallels, not copies. Just as the richness of Lean's work lies in what meets the eye, the richness of this study by Michael Anderegg lies especially in its detailed analysis of visual influences upon Lean's transformations. Especially as the discussions of the Dickens films demonstrate, Lean has done far more than "add pictures"; for, as Anderegg points out, "a film, in the act of re-creating it, inevitably destroys a literary text."

Final important evidence from Lean's "self-portrait" about the nature of his genius is his explanation that after making *Lawrence of Arabia* and *Dr. Zhivago* with scriptwriter Robert Bolt, they decided to "try an original"

(*Ryan's Daughter*). Anderegg's final chapter analyzes the unsatisfactory results: what the film conspicuously lacks is "a great statement" (not necessarily a sound or true statement, but a passionate utterance about the human condition). While admirably self-critical, Lean also finally displays a somewhat vindicating self-indulgence in his closing remark in the self-portrait. He says that, while occasionally the arts have produced a Shakespeare or a Beethoven, "we haven't produced anybody like that in the movies." Perhaps not, but the comparisons are excessively demanding; in their own art, directors like Griffith, Renoir, Bergman, and Fellini surely bear comparison with such immortals as Rubens or William Blake or Claude Debussy. One element that Michael Anderegg repeatedly stresses in Lean's work is the ambiguity in the stories he chooses. Like others distrustful of prophetic voices, he may not acknowledge the limits of his own practicality.

W. F.

Preface

DAVID LEAN is one of the world's most famous directors, but very few people, I suspect, could name all fifteen of his films or characterize his work with any precision. A quick glance over Lean's filmography suggests a director with no particular center of interest or coherent vision. Literary adaptations like *Great Expectations* and *Oliver Twist* rub elbows with so-called women's films like *Brief Encounter* and *Summer Madness* and with all-male adventures like *Bridge on the River Kwai* and *Lawrence of Arabia*. A close look at the films themselves, however, reveals unsuspected patterns. Stylistic and thematic motifs recur with surprising frequency among quite unrelated genres. Most of Lean's films, in fact, fall into two large categories: adventure and romance. The adventure films include *In Which We Serve, The Sound Barrier, Bridge on the River Kwai,* and *Lawrence of Arabia*. Among the romances are *Brief Encounter, Madeleine, The Passionate Friends, Summer Madness, Doctor Zhivago,* and *Ryan's Daughter*. The first group concentrates on the world of men, and the second group on the world, or at least the consciousness, of women. But even this distinction turns out to be superficial. Nearly all of his films have at their center a passionate intelligence: in Lean's hands, adventure and romance are very much the same thing.

Lean's major protagonists, whether male or female, seek to transform their lives by imposing their deepest imaginings on the "ordinary universe." Mostly, they fail. If they succeed, the success is so ambiguous as to resemble failure. T. E. Lawrence and Madeleine Smith, Colonel Nicholson and Laura Jesson, Ridgefield and Rosy Ryan are siblings under the skin: each seeks to break through the barriers of conventional thought and feeling, of morality and custom, of human limitations and human weakness, to some higher, more intense, deeply felt existence. Even the films that do not fit clearly into either category share these thematic concerns: one thinks of Pip's nameless yearnings in *Great Expectations*, Queenie Gibbons's rebellion in *This Happy Breed*, and Maggie Hobson's powerful will in *Hobson's Choice*.

Lean's films are united as well by stylistic preoccupations. Often praised for careful attention to precise atmospheric detail, Lean has always qualified his "realist" tendencies with a nonrealistic, mannered, expressionist visual style, from the slow-motion "drownings" of *In Which We Serve* to the impossibly verdant, overripe woods where Ryan's daughter makes love to her dream hero. The tilted camera angles of *Brief Encounter* and *Oliver Twist*; the studiously frozen surfaces of *Doctor Zhivago*; the complex narrative movements of *The Passionate Friends*; the disturbing sand formations of *Lawrence of Arabia*; the gothic atmospherics at the beginning of *Hobson's Choice*; the visual mystification of *Madeleine*: these are signs of an artist whose allegiance is not primarily to realism but to an inner, subjective vision. For so commercial a director, Lean is surprisingly prone to violate the accepted tenets of mainstream film technique, which strive to efface style in favor of transparent immediacy. Lean's style, far from effacing itself, reinforces and gives expression to the intense subjectivity of his male and female protagonists.

In Lean's first-person narratives—*Brief Encounter, Great Expectations, The Passionate Friends, Doctor Zhivago*—the subjectivity is an essential part of the fiction, but even the films that lack an explicit narrator or narrative voice are nevertheless "narrated" in a subjective fashion: *Lawrence of Arabia* is one long flashback that "belongs," presumably, to the mourners we see at Lawrence's funeral in the film's first sequence; *Madeleine* begins in the present and takes us into the past via an anonymous narrative voice; *This Happy Breed* seems to be narrated by the house at 17 Sycamore Road, Clapham Common; the flashbacks of *In Which We Serve* represent the collective consciousness of a ship's crew; and much of *Ryan's Daughter* and *Oliver Twist* emanates from the consciousness of their eponymous protagonists. Lean time and again strives against the objective tendency of film representation in order to make films that point to the inwardness of human experience.

In discussing Lean's films, I balance several obligations. I treat all of the films as independent entities while at the same time making connections among them; I focus on David Lean's directorial style without ignoring aspects of each film that may be completely extrinsic to his conscious decisions; I treat the films as aesthetic objects while attempting to see them as social products. Some films, undeniably, point to concerns outside themselves more urgently than do others, but every film, as Christian Metz reminds us, "is the site of a (more or less) productive encounter between the cinema and that which is not the cinema." As Metz further notes, one should not "panic at the thought of getting out of the domain of the cinema."[1] I therefore allow each film to create its own context without, I hope, abdicating responsibility for judgment. I have further attempted, when appropriate, to place Lean's films within the complex and frustrating history of the British cinema. Here, however, space limitations have dictated a cursory approach. The Selected Bibliography and Notes and References point the reader to more detailed information. I have dispensed almost entirely with merely personal allusions to Lean's private life, restricting myself to actions and events that have some bearing on his film-making career.

MICHAEL A. ANDEREGG

University of North Dakota

Acknowledgments

ONCE AGAIN, I owe special debts of gratitude to Pat Sheehan, Barbara Humphreys, David Parker, and Joe Balian at the Library of Congress Motion Pictures Division; film scholars could not ask for friendlier cooperation or more knowledgeable help. I also want to thank the staffs of the Charles K. Feldman Library at UCLA, the American Film Institute Library, and the Margaret Herrick Library of the Academy of Motion Picture Arts and Sciences.

The University of North Dakota provided a developmental leave and two Faculty Research Grants that made much of the writing of this book possible.

Special thanks to Laurence Goldstein, the editor of the *Michigan Quarterly Review*, for permission to reprint the substance of an essay on *Lawrence of Arabia* that first appeared there.

In addition to typing the manuscript with her usual intelligence and skill, Ursula Hovet exhibited interest and enthusiasm above and beyond the call of duty. Warren French, for the second time, has been a supportive and patient editor.

Jeanne Anderegg read and commented on various drafts of my manuscript; in doing so, she has saved me from innumerable infelicities of thought and style. Her support and encouragement cannot be adequately acknowledged or compensated.

Chronology

1908	David Lean born in Croydon, England, 25 March, the son of Francis William le Blount and Helena Annie (Tangye) Lean.
1920–1925	Educated at Leighton Park School, a Quaker institution in Reading.
1927	Employed by Gaumont Pictures at Gainsborough Studios as a clapper boy and all-around "gofer."
1928–1930	Works as cutting-room assistant, camera assistant, and third assistant director.
1930	Becomes chief editor for Gaumont British News.
1931–1933	Becomes editor for British Movietone News and Paramount British News.
1934	Edits "Quota Quickies" for Paramount.
1935	Edits his first important feature film, Paul Czinner's *Escape Me Never.*
1936	Edits Czinner's *As You Like It.*
1938–1939	Edits *Pygmalion* for Anthony Asquith and Leslie Howard and *French Without Tears* for Asquith.
1940	Marries actress Kay Walsh (divorced, 1949).
1941–1942	Edits *The Invaders (The 49th Parallel)* and *One of Our Aircraft Is Missing* for Powell and Pressburger; edits and assists in the direction of *Major Barbara* for Gabriel Pascal.
1942	Codirects *In Which We Serve* with Noel Coward.
1943	Forms, in association with J. Arthur Rank, an independent production company, Cineguild, with Ronald Neame, Coward, and Anthony Havelock-Allan.
1944	*This Happy Breed.*

1945 *Blithe Spirit* and *Brief Encounter*; becomes first British director to be nominated for an American Academy Award (for *Brief Encounter*).

1946 Directs *Great Expectations*, which wins three Academy Awards.

1948 *Oliver Twist*; release of this film in the United States is postponed because of charges of anti-Semitism.

1949 *The Passionate Friends*; marries Ann Todd (divorced, 1957).

1950 *Madeleine*; Cineguild dissolved; joins Alexander Korda's London Films.

1952 Produces and directs *The Sound Barrier.*

1954 Produces and directs *Hobson's Choice.*

1955 *Summer Madness*; Korda's British Lion goes bankrupt.

1957 Directs *The Bridge on the River Kwai*, which wins seven Academy Awards, including best director.

1960 Marries Leila Devi (divorced, 1978); begins production on *Lawrence of Arabia.*

1962 *Lawrence of Arabia* released, wins seven "Oscars," including best director.

1965 *Doctor Zhivago.*

1966–1969 Various projects are announced and then dropped, including "The Slave" with Julie Christie, "The Battle of Berlin," and "Galileo."

1970 *Ryan's Daughter*; a retrospective of Lean's films held at the Museum of Modern Art, October 29 through November 3.

1971 "Tale of Two Cities" and "Gandhi" announced.

1973 Presented with the D. W. Griffith Award from the Directors Guild of America.

1977 "Captain Bligh and Mr. Christian" announced as his next project.

1981 *Variety* announces that Lean is to film E. M. Forster's *A Passage to India.*

1984 Principal photography begins on *A Passage to India.*

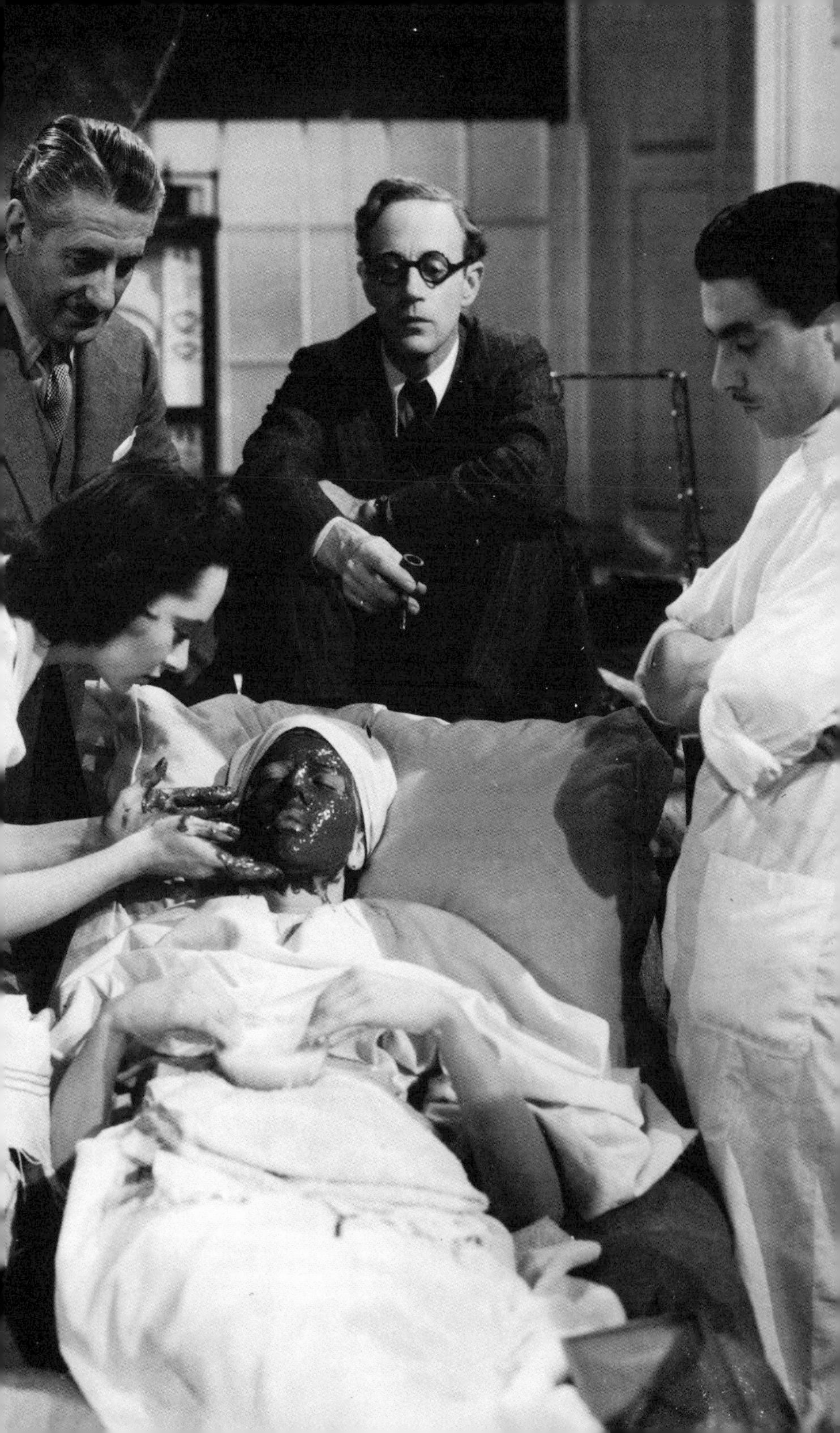

1

Beginnings

DAVID LEAN began his film career at the age of nineteen as a bottom-rung apprentice for the Gaumont-British company at London's Gainsborough Studios. The son of strict Quakers, Lean had been encouraged by his father to study accounting, but he soon discovered that his interests lay elsewhere, and spent most of his spare time at the movies. "I was fascinated by films," he would later recall, "but it took me a long time to realize that one could actually work in them."[1] One is less surprised by Lean's youthful naiveté than by his having had the courage to give up a secure career in accounting for something as chancy as the British film industry. His arrival at Gainsborough in 1927 coincided with one of the worst of the periodic, seemingly inevitable crises that plagued British films. The year 1926 had been disastrous: the amount of screen time devoted to British films in British cinemas, which had been steadily shrinking since the end of World War I, had dwindled to 5 percent. "By 1927," according to a government report, "the British film industry was well on the way to extinction."[2] Lean was presumably unaware of or undeterred by the bleak prospects ahead.

The sad plight of British films was in large part the result of American economic imperialism. "The Americans," as historian Michael Chanan notes, "had achieved a dominant position in distribution, and employed certain distributive malpractices (known as block booking and blind booking) which effectively kept British films off the screen."[3] The British government, responding to the crisis, intervened with the Cinematograph Films Act of 1927, which abolished blind and block booking and imposed on both film renters and exhibitors "the obligation to acquire and show respectively, a minimum proportion, or quota, of British films in respect of the foreign films acquired and exhibited."[4] The effect of what came to be known as the (First) Quota Act was dramatic. Only twenty-six British feature films were produced in 1926; by 1929, the number had risen to 128. But a dark shadow qualified this seemingly bright picture: many of these films were inexpensive concoctions hastily thrown together to satisfy

Leslie Howard and Wendy Hiller in Pygmalion, *a film edited by David Lean and directed by Howard and Anthony Asquith (1938).*

the quota obligations of foreign renters. If these "quota quickies" did nothing to improve the status of British films, however, they did provide a training ground for a number of future directors like Alfred Hitchcock and David Lean.

At Gainsborough, Lean underwent a varied apprenticeship. Initially attached to a unit filming Maurice Elvey's *Quinneys* (1927), his job was to hold up the number board in front of the camera at the beginning of each "take." Subsequently, he worked as a camera assistant and as a third assistant director, the latter job consisting almost entirely of carrying tea and calling actors onto the set. However, his interests soon focused on the editing process. After watching the cutting of *The Night Porter* (Sewell Collins,1930), an early sound film, he became a cutting-room assistant. He was made a full-fledged editor while working on newsreels and by 1930 he had been promoted to chief editor of Gaumont British News reputedly at only five shillings a week (about $1.25).[5] Over the next several years (1931–33), Lean performed the same function for both British Movietone News and Paramount British News.

British newsreels of the 1930s were in many ways characteristic of British filmmaking as a whole. Five companies held a virtual newsreel monopoly. Lean worked for the three largest of these, of which two (British Movietone News and Paramount British News) were owned by American film companies, a situation reflecting Ernest Betts's observation that "the most striking fact about the British film industry is that it is not British."[6] From the outset of his career, Lean was trained in American methods and paid with American money. At the same time, he was exposed to the innate conservatism of the British cinema. As Rachel Low has shown, "The newsreel companies worked together to a considerable extent to avoid arousing antagonisms which might have led to demands for censorship. They maintained some similarity in style and content."[7] Put another way, these "newsreels" ignored news as much as possible, concentrating instead on flower shows, sports events, and royal progresses. The commentators, Low adds, "told us what we were looking at rather than what it meant, and subtly moulded our attitudes by their very correct respect for established authority, their irreproachable sentiments at natural or man-made disasters, their hearty self-assurance, their bland confidence that all would yet be well."[8] Since Lean, in addition to cutting the film, sometimes wrote and spoke the commentary, he must share some of the blame for the generally innocuous content of British newsreels.

Lean did not continue long with newsreels, however. In 1934, Paramount moved him over to its feature film division, and he began to edit "quota quickies." It was here that he met Merrill White, an American who had been chief cutter for Ernest Lubitsch. "I learned all about [editing] from Merrill White," Lean would claim many years later.[9] White must have been a good teacher, for Lean soon earned a reputation as one of the best editors in England and Paramount offered to let him direct as well as edit some of its low-budget films. But Lean chose to bide his time; quota quickies could easily become a director's graveyard—one failure and there was no second chance. Besides, he enjoyed editing: "It's so peaceful. The film. A moviola. A pair of scissors and a quiet room with no pressures."[10] Furthermore, though Lean may not have been fully aware of this at the time, the British film industry was about to enter a new "boom" period that would provide opportunities for a first-class editor. The international success of Alexander Korda's *Private Life of Henry VIII* (something of a fluke, as it turned out) brought new prestige to British films as well as an aura of success to filmmakers with foreign accents (Korda was Hungarian). One of these, the transplanted German director Paul Czinner, gave Lean his first chance to edit a class "A" film with *Escape Me Never* (1936). Lean went on to edit Czinner's next two films, *As You Like It* (1936) and *Dreaming Lips* (1937).

The boom period turned out to be shortlived, and by the time Lean had become Britain's best-known and highest-paid editor the industry was once again facing crisis. Although film output had risen to 212 in 1936 and 228 by 1937, most of these films were quota quickies made entirely for home consumption. The only chance British films had to become financially viable, however, was to break into overseas markets, and this they signally failed to do. Attempts to beat Hollywood at its own game resulted in costly, overproduced failures. Even successful films were of little help, since the structure of the industry guaranteed that a large share of the profits went to distributors rather than being rechanneled into production. A number of companies were faced with bankruptcy, including Lean's first employer, Gaumont-British, which ceased making feature films, and Alexander Korda's London Films. In 1938, Korda's Denham Studios were acquired by the millionaire mill-owner J. Arthur Rank. Once again, however, the government intervened. A new Quota Act came into force on 1 April 1938, which maintained the quota system but at the same time established a minimum cost test (£7,500—about $37,500, still remarkably low by Hollywood standards) for quota films, thereby eliminating—in theory, at least—the "quickies." The new act also encouraged American companies to make films in England. Whether the Quota Act together with new American money and talent would have brought an end to the crisis of the late 1930s is now impossible to determine. World War II intervened, affecting the film industry as profoundly as it affected everything else.

The war, as it turned out, gave Lean the opportunity he was looking for. Having established himself in the industry by editing some of the most important British films of the late 1930s and early 1940s—including *Pyg-*

malion (1938), *French Without Tears* (1939), *Major Barbara* (1941), *The 49th Parallel* (1941), and *One of Our Aircraft Is Missing* (1942)—Lean was asked by Noel Coward to help with the latter's debut as a film producer-director. Playwright, composer, actor, director, and producer, Coward (1899–1973) was one of England's supreme entertainers, a spokesman for and symbol of the witty, gay, frivolous, upper-class London of the 1920s and 1930s. Initially quite reluctant to involve himself seriously in the cinema, a medium marginal to his interests (although he had played a small role in D. W. Griffith's *Hearts of the World* [1918] and had starred, notably, in Charles MacArthur and Ben Hecht's *The Scoundrel* [1935]), Coward was talked into producing, writing, directing, and starring in a patriotic war film by Filippo del Guidice, one of a number of somewhat eccentric immigrants who contributed colorful if brief chapters to the history of British films. Always shrewd in his estimate both of public taste and of his own talents, Coward protected his new project by engaging the help of someone with a complete grasp of film technique. The choice of Lean, himself a beginner behind the camera, was perfect from Coward's point of view: he could take advantage of an experienced technician without having to accommodate the ego of an established filmmaker. Thus it was that David Lean became co-director of *In Which We Serve* (1942), "one of the crucial films in the history of the British cinema."[11]

2

Interpreting Noel Coward

In Which We Serve (1942)

"*IN WHICH WE SERVE* by Noel Coward"; "Captain Kinross—Noel Coward"; "Music by Noel Coward"; "Produced by Noel Coward"; "Directed by Noel Coward and David Lean." The title cards for *In Which We Serve* leave us little room to question whose film we are watching, and what follows does not significantly contradict the promise of the credits. As actor, author, and general impresario, Noel Coward pervades the film's very texture. He developed the screenplay from the wartime experiences of his friend Lord Louis Mountbatten, commander of the HMS *Kelly,* a destroyer lost in the battle of Crete on 21 May 1941. The opportunity to make a direct and significant contribution to the war effort (more or less expected of everyone in wartime Britain) could not have come at a better time. Coward's previous role as a sort of unofficial good-will ambassador to the United States had been met with derision in the British press. Lord Beaverbrook's *Sunday Express*, in particular, was quick to criticize: "Mr. Coward is not the man for the job. His flippant England—cocktails, countesses, caviare—has gone."[1] (Coward got his revenge on Beaverbrook: *In Which We Serve* includes a shot of a copy of the *Daily Express* bearing the unprescient headline "No War This Year.") *In Which We Serve* was for Coward a personal vindication.

Given the nature of film and the complexities of collaboration, separating out Lean's contribution from Coward's becomes a difficult task. The film does provide some hints, however. When the credits end and the narrative begins, the hand of an editor immediately asserts itself. The opening montage sequence depicting the building of the destroyer HMS *Torrin* (by extension, any ship) draws upon both the British Documentary School and the style and format of the newsreel departments where Lean developed his editing skills. *In Which We Serve* begins with a documentary of work that counterpoints the mutual dependence of men and material, an illustration of the general ("This is the story of a ship"), a montage that asserts the cinematic. This is a Noel Coward *film* (not a play disguised

Top: John Mills and Kay Walsh in In Which We Serve. *Bottom:* In Which We Serve: *British troops come home from Dunkirk.*

as a film), but also a filmmaker's film, David Lean's film. Though we cannot precisely determine Lean's contribution, his presence makes itself felt, especially in retrospect. We can see in *In Which We Serve* not only standard Coward ingredients—understated patriotism; class humor; episodic structuring; sentimentality raised to a pitch of genuine feeling; a condescending, somewhat tongue-in-cheek view of the lower orders—but several Lean concerns as well: the tension between the public and the personal, the repression of emotion; the obsessional nature of the military personality. In the character of Captain Kinross, too, we detect more than a hint of the excessive intensity of a Colonel Nicholson or a T. E. Lawrence.

Coward and Lean together hit upon a tone and style exactly suited to the needs of wartime Britain. Earlier British war films had enjoyed little sucess either in raising morale at home or in pleading Britain's cause abroad. Several notable documentaries emerged soon after the outbreak of war, but these had minimal distribution and were of limited appeal. The fiction film, for its part, seldom came to grips with the hard issues posed by the German threat. Films like *The Lion Has Wings* (1939), *Contraband* (1940), *Night Train to Munich* (1940), and *Dangerous Moonlight* (1941), whatever their virtues as art or entertainment, contributed little of substance to Britain's propaganda needs, either striking a foolish note of complacency or treating the war on the level of a 1930s spy thriller (Carol Reed's *Night Train to Munich* was virtually a remake of Hitchcock's *The Lady Vanishes* [1938]). Such films, by all accounts, had a negligible effect on American public opinion or policy, a crucial matter in the years 1939–1941. Some sympathetic American observers expressed frustration at Britain's failure to project a self-image comprehensible in the United States.[2] *In Which We Serve* was hailed in America as "the first really great picture of World War II"[3] and "one of the most eloquent motion pictures of this or any other time."[4] The film manages to glorify the fighting spirit of Britain while giving memorable expression to the stiff-upper-lip, "thumbs up" ethos some Americans frequently find distasteful.

In Which We Serve very much reflects a particular historical moment and, consequently, film historians often dismiss it as no more than a mirror of its time. Real or imagined flaws are attributed to "context"; historical perspective is summoned to explain what appears to the commentator as dated or naive. So we read, for example, that *In Which We Serve* belongs to "a period of history when no one spoke about 'anti'-war films," and that it represents "the simplified way in which all people then looked at war."[5] *The Oxford Companion to Film,* for its part, explains that the film's "unquestioning acceptance of the existing social order is usually embarrassing to an audience not subject to the original conditions of crisis."[6] Such comments are not only unnecessary, they also fail correctly to gauge the relationship between film and society. Quite apart from a simplistic historicism, both views wrongly assume that films merely reflect, rather than shape, attitudes. Indeed, far from regarding war in a "simplified way," the British people in mid-1942, when *In Which We Serve* was in production, were exhibiting an alarmingly low morale. Brendan Bracken, the British Minister of Information, expressed grave concern in his monthly reports to the Cabinet. According to his analysis, there was a general "loss of interest in the war and in war news; there were grievances about disparities between servicemen's pay and that of civilian war workers. . . . There was a feeling that a lack of a proper spirit of patriotism among some sections of the female population was keeping men back from dangerous duty."[7] If we consider the context, we can see that *In Which We Serve* wants its viewers to think a certain way about such matters as war and class and duty and courage. This is a far cry from merely reflecting the public mood.

From this standpoint, we can appreciate how *In Which We Serve* works to turn an atmosphere of defeat and despair into one of hope and victory. In a key sequence, the HMS *Torrin* aids in rescuing the British Expeditionary Force off the Dunkirk beaches. The film—logically, in terms of its focus—emphasizes the *Torrin*'s (the navy's, Britain's) success in pulling off the rescue, not the army's (Britain's) failure that required a rescue in the first place. Coward helps to create the myth whereby Dunkirk comes "to stand for the way in which, in the face of adversity, all classes of the community worked long hours in the national interest."[8] Defeat thus becomes victory. But the film does not ignore the darker meaning of Dunkirk. Coward and Lean create a calculated, tactful sequence set on the Dover docks and culminating in a long tracking shot of the rescued soldiers' faces as they prepare to march off to fight another day. Their expressions reflect a somber awareness of defeat tempered by courage and determination. This balance of loss and gain informs the entire film. Coward's story, after all, is about defeat: the *Torrin* is destroyed by the enemy. The film does not assume that "our side" must inevitably win; rather it exhorts us, in its understated way, to work courageously to that end. Like another British war film of 1942, Cavalcanti's *Went the Day Well?*, which begins with a prologue set in the future, *after* Hitler's defeat, but then shows in flashback how easily, in fact, Britain could lose, *In Which We Serve* is a cautionary tale, a warning as well as an affirmation.

Not surprisingly, *In Which We Serve* stresses cohesion and unity, a sense of shared purpose and shared dangers. This explains why, as in William Wyler's *Mrs. Miniver* (1942), great stress is placed on how war affects the home front. As in that American film, it is to the civilians among the major characters that death comes, and in particular to the women: the men, for the most part, survive. They also serve (and die) who only stand and wait. This mood obliterates class divisions, condemning complacency but generally ignoring "politics" beyond the most straightforward of formulations: "world domination—that's what the little rat's after," someone says of Hitler. No deeper issues are sought for. War is a given, an inevitability. Only momentarily, almost imperceptibly, and usually with humor, does any other view emerge, as when Shorty Blake responds to Chamberlain's radio announcement regretting the painful necessity of declaring war with, "Well, it ain't exactly a bank 'oliday for us." Chamberlain, of course, is a safe target. Nevertheless, a point is made. The politicians have gotten us into this mess; the ordinary man and woman fight and die. Even such a small wedge as this tempers the too easy acceptance of "things as they are" that the film-work so skillfully elicits.

In developing its structural and thematic strategies, *In Which We Serve* borrows elements from Coward's patriotic panorama *Calvacade* (1931) and from *This Happy Breed*, a play he had been working on before the war and which he and Lean would film in 1944. The film unfolds as a series of flashback memories of crew members on the *Torrin* as they hang on to a life raft, their ship having been shot out from under them. As his protagonists, Coward chooses types representative of the British class structure. Captain Kinross, or "D" as he is known to his men (played by Coward himself), stands in for the upper-middle-class, stiff-upper-lip officer; Walter Hardy (Bernard Miles), the ship's chief petty officer, is from the lower middle class; Ordinary Seaman "Shorty" Blake (John Mills) has a working-class background. The message, of course, is, "We're all in this together"; the HMS *Torrin* berths a cross-section of British society. (In many American war films, Polish-, Italian-, and Irish-Americans fill out the platoon; the point is similar, though the markers of potential conflict are quite different.) Neither the film's structuring nor the arrangement of characters along class lines is as schematic in practice as my description would suggest. *In Which We Serve* has in fact a fluid, almost illogical structure. All of the early flashbacks are initiated with a shot of the sailor concerned, but as the film progresses this device is not consistently employed. Sometimes the flashback begins without introduction and simply ends at the life raft; some of the flashbacks involve minor characters (as with the young sailor played by Richard Attenborough). The flashback sequences can even intertwine with each other, starting with one character and picking up another, whose adventures the film then follows. Walter Hardy and Shorty Blake are related by marriage, so their stories quite naturally overlap; but there is no particular reason, except dramatic and thematic convenience, for Shorty and Freda (Kay Walsh), traveling on their honeymoon, to encounter the captain and his wife (Celia Johnson).

Given the structure of his script, Coward was wise to choose a former editor to help him direct. Lean more than likely bears the responsibility for the film's fluid and imaginative transitions, which help to unite the individual stories into a collective memory, a communal experience. The flashbacks, in effect, are the ship's; all of the men on board share the images of shore life and the memories of families left behind. Past and present are edited together as in a dream: Captain "D" summoning up memories as he slowly falls through the silent water; Shorty Blake's image of Freda in her wedding dress "floating" on the dark ocean. Lean's editing contributes as well to the film's tone of understatement. Shorty's courtship of Freda, for example, is given to us in one simple "cut": he says to her, "What's your name," and the next shot is an exterior of their train traveling through the night. Particularly effective in this context is the moment just before the battle when Lean cuts to the ship's doctor (James Donald) looking at the antiseptic instrument table he has just prepared. Such moments, of course, owe much of their expressiveness to framing, dialogue, performance, and so forth; editing simply underlines and facilitates the structural grace and narrative complexity characteristic of *In Which We Serve*.

The balance between the credits, which so clearly proclaim Coward's auteur-ship, and the film's first sequence, which just as surely points to Lean, maintains itself throughout. The documentary style of the shipbuilding montage does not, however, reappear. Coward's highly stylized screenplay, carefully structured through oppositions and contrasts—past and present, war and peace, the general and the particular, a constricted setting and a wide scope, upper- and lower-class behavior—hardly aims at documentary realism. And yet the film's style frequently papers over the script's deliberate patterning, lending a pseudodocumentary surface to a highly schematic foundation. The project of *In Which We Serve* is to keep in careful balance the typical and the particular, to provide representative figures (Captain "D," Number One, Doctor, "Flaps," "Guns," "Torps," etc.) with human individuality. The film's fusion of realism and stylization can be seen in the way Coward, Lean, cinematographer Ronald Neame, and art director David Rawnsley construct the battle sequences. Rawnsley designed a flexible, evocative, minimalist set for the *Torrin*'s superstructure. Though the ship is clearly a sound-stage mock-up, the intercutting between the captain's bridge and stock shots of airplanes and ocean is carefully controlled to provide a counterpoint among studio footage, live action, and models that seems perfectly right. In the film's climactic battle, the continuous overpass of German bombers is truly frightening, the very fragility of Rawnsley's mock-up ship contributing to the impresssion of vulnerability. The camera's almost constant movement in these sequences helps to link shots very different both in content and provenance in a manner that further reinforces the tension between objective and subjective realities.

In Which We Serve benefits as well from a number of particularly fine performances. John Mills, Bernard Miles, Kay Walsh, Joyce Cary, and Celia Johnson all imbue rather typical characters with carefully nuanced individuality. Alix Kinross's Christmas dinner speech, as movingly interpreted by Celia Johnson, ideally combines brave and conventional words on the lot of a sailor's wife with a modulated emotional coloration that signifies the suppression of conflicting feelings. The decision not to break up her speech with reaction shots intensifies the emotional resonance. Coward's understated script gives the actors something to work against. Several extremely moving scenes—the three women subjected to the Blitz; Shorty Blake telling Walter Hardy that the latter's wife has been killed; Alix Kinross and Freda Blake learning that their husbands have survived—depend for their impact on the established tension between feeling and its suppression. Ironically, only Coward's performance seems in a number of ways off-key. It is, of course, in the character of Captain "D" that the stiff-upper-lip attitude receives its definitive expression ("the British cinema," Lindsay Anderson once wrote, "has never recovered from Noel Coward as Captain 'D' "[9]), but even though that is how author Coward wrote the part ("You all did pretty well," the captain tells his crew after they have courageously survived a harrowing encounter with the enemy), actor Coward increases the distance between us and the character, almost as if he were afraid of striking even the slightest irresponsible, "Noel-Cowardish" note. In the end, however, Coward very nearly recoups his losses: the hint of emotion in his delivery of Kinross's farewell speech to his men moves us in part because he has been previously so unbending. In these final moments, Coward's performance releases, as the film does throughout, "an unhesitating current of emotional solidarity which reaches all the way to the audience,"[10] transcending at once the barriers of class, the limits of propaganda, and the artifice of fiction.

Noel Coward, not surprisingly, received the lion's share of credit for the success of *In Which We Serve;* Lean's name was hard to find either on promotional material or in the reviews. But Coward, for one, valued Lean's contribution. "Well, dear boy," he told Lean when *In Which We Serve* was finished, "you can take anything I write and make a film of it." Lean accepted the offer, forming a company with Anthony Havelock-Allan and Ronald Neame (the associate producer and cinematographer, respectively, of *In Which We Serve*) for the purpose of filming Coward's plays. Their company, Cineguild, joined a cluster of production companies formed under the umbrella of the Rank organization and collectively known as Independent Producers. Among others were the Archers (Michael Powell and Emeric Pressburger), Individual (Frank Launder and Sidney Gilliat), and Wessex (Ian Dalrymple). As a group, independent Producers played a major part in the wartime and immediate postwar "renaissance" of the British cinema and contributed as well to Rank's strategy for penetrating the ever-elusive American market. Cineguild's first two films, *This Happy Breed* and *Blithe Spirit,* were filmed in color for prestige value at a time when there were only four Technicolor cameras in Great Britain. Rank's efforts had mixed results: Laurence Olivier's *Henry V* (1944) and *Brief Encounter* (1945), Lean's fourth and last collaboration with Coward, were quite successful and added significantly to the reputation of British films; Gabriel Pascal's *Caesar and Cleopatra* (1945), on the other hand, was a critical and financial disaster. Although they made Rank little money, *This Happy Breed* and *Blithe Spirit* contributed modestly to a general sense that the British cinema had come of age.

This Happy Breed (1944)

In his play *This Happy Breed* (first staged in 1943), which traces episodically the fortunes of a "typical" family during a crucial period of British history, Noel Coward tried to achieve for the lower middle classes what he had for the upper classes in *Calvacade* over a decade earlier. Coward follows the Gibbons family through the interwar years 1919–1939, from the moment Frank and Ethel move into their new house at 17 Sycamore Road, Clapham Common, to the moment they move out again some twenty years later. Compared to *Calvacade,* however, *This Happy Breed* seems undernourished. This was perhaps inevitable, considering the step down in class: we could hardly expect the equivalent of seaside resorts, elegant restaurants, and cruises on the *Titanic* for the Gibbons family. *Calvacade* was an extravaganza in twenty-one scenes set in over a dozen different locations; *This Happy Breed,* in nine scenes, unfolds entirely in the dining room of the Gibbons house. The difference undoubtedly reflects, as well, the austerity of the 1943 theater season in contrast to the more extravagant West End of 1931. *This Happy Breed,* furthermore, was clearly born of the immediate pressures of wartime, whereas *Calvacade* sprung from a more reflective historical moment. The later play, as a result, now seems somewhat contrived and polemical in its attempt to render the indomitable spirit of the common English people, though at the time it struck a responsive chord in a London that had endured constant and punishing German bombardment with dignity and courage.

Reduced to the bare bones of their structure, Coward's play and the nearly identical screenplay he wrote for the film unfold as a series of more or less cruel domestic jokes: mother-in-law jokes (mother-in-law problems would seem to be *the* middle-class disorder in Coward's plays: see his one-act *Fumed Oak*), spinster jokes, shrewish-wife jokes, drinking-husband jokes, erring-daughter jokes, and so forth. Coward frequently condescends to his characters, drawing their problems and small triumphs from so many bundles of clichés. When dealing with an upper- and upper-middle-class milieu, Coward can transform the constant follies of human behavior into a kind of wild eccentricity; his Gibbonses and his Mitchells, alas, do not have the luxury of idiosyncracy: their class, it would seem,

Robert Newton and Celia Johnson in This Happy Breed.

severely limits their self-expression. Frank and Ethel Gibbons act out a predictable dynamic. Ethel is rational, undemonstrative, pious, unaesthetic; Frank is emotional, warm, skeptical, and devoted to the pleasures of gardening. To this extent, one could say that Coward reverses sex-role expectations. Turning a cliché on its head, however, simply creates another cliché. Both characters are predictable because neither is much more than the sum of these characteristics. That Coward's text nevertheless "works" in certain specific ways testifies to the cleverness of his dramatic structuring and his ability simultaneously to satirize and reinforce the mores and behavior of his characters so that both the play and the screenplay constantly seesaw between comedy and sentiment.

Coward's text achieves dramatic interest through a process of allowing anomalies to emerge from its lower-middle-class milieu and then absorbing them back into the original fabric, which remains undisturbed. Any fissures that develop are quickly and effectively filled in. *This Happy Breed* both condemns complacency—the attitude that "everything in the garden's lovely"—and becomes an instance of it. The text can thus indulge in the luxury of questioning itself without threatening an ultimate reintegration. We feel that various political, social, and psychological complexes are explored when they have been introduced merely to reinforce the dominant ideology in a dramatically convincing manner. The treatment of young Sam Leadbitter provides the most obvious instance of this process. Sam, an incipient Marxist ("a bit of a Bolshie"), expresses a necessary reminder of social and political facts and sentiments that, given its scope and purpose, inevitably colors the text. At the same time, Sam is something of a fool, easily dismissed by the other characters, who find him "cockeyed," or "soft," or, with Frank, simply immature: "He'll grow out of it. I used to shoot me neck off to beat the band when I was his age." Frank's response both incorporates and dismisses Sam, and hence his point of view, in one breath. And the text does the same thing: Sam marries the elder Gibbons daughter and settles down ("He had a nice look at the Labour Government and saw what a mess they was making of everything. . . . He's Britain for ever now all right"). "There's always something to be said for everything" becomes the perfect bromide, suggesting as it does—and as it is meant to do—that there is very little to be said for most things. Coward's strategy has its dangers, however, since in performance the anomalies may be so intensely rendered that they resist the text's attempt to neutralize them. The film, as we shall see, pushes several of these anomalies into the foreground and as a consequence disturbs the careful balance of Coward's text.

Considered simply as an adaptation, the film *This Happy Breed* seems remarkably faithful to the play it adapts, which is only to say that the verbal text is incorporated into the film with only minor modifications: Noel Coward's presence as producer-screenwriter insures this. In one way, then, the film is first and foremost a performance of the play. In practice, however, David Lean's film is something more than the effective realization of a preexisting text. His direction (with or without Coward's full participation and awareness) brings pressure to bear on the text's unexamined (or underexamined) premises. In particular, the film opens up a discussion of the place of women in the bourgeois family with such an intensity that Coward's text no longer succeeds in containing the disturbance it has posed.

Before considering Lean's emphases in detail, it should be acknowledged that the conscientious transfer of a play-text to the screen involves a number of more or less automatic effects and operations that in themselves can modify the meaning of the original. Certain theatrical conventions, for example, cannot be carried into a film without becoming transformed. Specifically, the various conventions of the single-set, "realistic," well-made play affect time and space in a particular way. Certain "absences"—places and characters and activities we hear about but never see—are incorporated and justified by the medium's formal requirements. In film, however, a medium theoretically able to "show everything," such absences become problematical. What we do not see becomes as important as what we do see. In the theater, of course, theatrical convention and theme have a tendency to reinforce each other. That the entire action of *This Happy Breed* unfolds in the Gibbons dining room is more than a matter of dramatic economy (although it is that as well): the play's setting intensifies its thematic and dramatic emphasis on the biological family. On the stage, too, absence can have its impact: why is it, for example, that although the next-door neighbor, Bob Mitchell, constantly pops over, his wife, Nora, is never seen? Nevertheless, the film makes us much more aware—makes it more of an issue—that we are spending most of our time in a restricted space (even though the film, unlike the play, occasionally carries us elsewhere): we are conscious of all that we do not see. The Gibbons house takes on a dominating, nearly claustrophobic presence, alerting us to the dark side of all the positive values associated with hearth and home.

As if aware of these implications, Lean does in fact "open up" Coward's play with atmospheric inserts placed at points equivalent to the play's scene breaks. These provide transitions, filling in the sometimes large temporal breaks and covering the fissures Coward's structure requires. We are thus treated to a mosaic of cultural, social, and political events—the British Empire Exhibit, the General Strike, a Charleston competition, the arrival of the talkies, George V's funeral, Chamberlain's return from Munich—to which the play, if it takes note of them at all, only alludes in passing. These inserts enrich the film's texture (introducing, in a sense, the epic manner of *Calvacade*) and heighten the social context without diluting the emphasis on the family in Clapham Common. More significantly, perhaps, Lean employs some of these transitional sequences to comment more directly than does the play on the implications of the events depicted. Particularly striking in this regard is the sequence that begins with an Armistice Day parade. As the sound of cheering dies down, the image of marching soldiers dissolves to a black and white still photo of soldiers in a muddy World War I battlefield while a plaintive, wistful melody plays on the soundtrack. The camera pulls back to reveal the photo as part of a poster advertising "Tickler's Tours of the Battlefields." Bridging a gap in time, Lean unites background and foreground (Tickler's is the travel agency where Frank Gibbons works), pausing long enough to comment strikingly and surprisingly on the unspoken implications of the parade we have just watched, and then shifting quickly to a light but pointed note of irony. Without violating the letter of Coward's text, Lean finds a filmic way of rendering a concept for which words alone would be both too much and too little.

For the most part, however, Lean "performs" Noel Coward's text, makes it operable. This is in no way an automatic process. Even when Lean seems to be doing nothing more than capturing as faithfully as possible an effective moment from the play, he modifies the form of expression. Consider, for example, the scene where Vi, the elder of the Gibbons daughters, has to tell her parents that her brother, Reg, has been killed in an auto accident. Lean adopts Coward's theatrical method—a method that depends, very particularly, on the meaning of what we do not see—while at the same time contributing a resonance only possible with film. In the film, as in the play, Vi pauses in the dining room as she prepares to tell her parents, who are both in the garden, of the accident. She exits through the ("upstage") French doors, leaving the room empty. As she leaves, the camera tracks slightly right to left, as if to follow her, and then stops. The only sound is the somewhat jazzy melody from the radio Reg had given his mother. After a pause, the camera begins to track slowly from left to right, at the same time panning toward the left, keeping the French doors in center frame while gradually revealing more of the garden, which is off left. The double movement of the camera seems to echo our own mixed feelings of curiosity and reticence, feelings reinforced by the refusal to cut, to *go* to the garden. Both camera movements stop as Ethel appears, followed by Frank. They enter the dining room, and Ethel moves to a chair and sits. Only now does Lean cut, framing the couple more tightly. Frank also sits, at the same time placing his hand on hers. The camera moves quickly back from them; the image fades to black. We have here a perfect example of the eloquence of offscreen space.

The performance of the text naturally includes—could not exist without—the performance of the actors. And it is with the actors in particular, with the performances they give and the images they project, that a subtext begins to emerge, a subtext that at times threatens to swamp the text proper. Celia Johnson and Kay Walsh (now David Lean's wife), especially, brightly illuminate corners of Coward's imaginative world that, one feels, were meant to remain in semidarkness. Most of the other members of Lean's generally excellent cast (John Mills, Stanley Holloway, Amy Veness) lend credence to characters only thinly developed by the text; in this sense, they help to support Coward's project. The casting of Robert Newton as the ordinary (and "ordinary looking") Frank Gibbons, on the other hand, sets up a mild tension between actor and character. Although Newton underplays beautifully, the eccentricities of his acting personality surface from time to time, modifying without ever quite undermining the ordinariness the script insists upon. Had he been given free rein (as he will be given in *Oliver Twist*, and as he was given by Laurence Olivier in *Henry V* the same year as *This Happy Breed*, in both films to good effect) the result would have been ludicrous. As it is, Newton walks a thin line, holding himself in check and yet making us aware that Frank Gibbons may not be as ordinary as all that.

A far greater tension, however, projects itself in Celia Johnson's performance as Ethel Gibbons. As Coward has conceived Ethel, her sharpness and constant scolding, her undemonstrative behavior, her role as upholder of what is "proper" and "fit," are simply externals of personality: beneath the surface is a strong, kind, sensitive woman. When their daughter, Queenie, runs away with a married man, Frank's response is to suggest that perhaps Queenie "couldn't help herself" whereas Ethel's response is to disown her ("I'll never forgive her to the end of my days"). By the play's end, of course, Ethel does forgive her daughter. This is meant to be touching just as Ethel's constant deflection of Frank's affectionate gestures is meant to be amusing. Celia Johnson's performance, however, covers Ethel with a dark and disturbing shadow. Johnson is particularly skilled at projecting tight-lipped, neurotic repression (which is why, no doubt, Coward and Lean were to use her in *Brief Encounter*, where she finds her ideal role). From the viewpoint of what the text wants to achieve, it could be argued that Johnson brings—and that Lean allows her to bring—perhaps too much conviction to her performance in *This Happy Breed*, thus throwing Coward's careful balancing act out of kilter by turning Ethel Gibbons into a somewhat harsh and unappealing character. Actually, Lean and Johnson simply carry Ethel to her logical and dramatic limits. Beneath the surface of this "typical" marriage, a sexually, emotionally, and perhaps even intellectually (the film's Ethel does not drop her "h's" or make grammatical errors as does the play's) dissatisfied woman is struggling to break out—or, rather, struggling not to break out—and the effect of the repression itself creates a subtextual but nevertheless powerful undertone.

With Queenie, the Gibbonses' younger daughter, the fissures Coward has worked into his text open up even more disturbingly. Queenie is the "bad" daughter, the rebel, and in a number of ways she is quite unpleasant and unsympathetic. She condescends to her parents because she finds them "common" and she is cruel to her faithful admirer, Bill (the boy next door), rejecting him for a married man presumably higher on the social ladder. A snob, she is vulgar in her snobbishness. And yet Coward gives Queenie such presence and forcefulness that she emerges as the most complex character in *This Happy Breed*. Coward, one feels, has drawn on something genuine in himself in creating her. Her dissatisfactions are heartfelt and her fears ring true. "How awful to be so dependent on a man living or dying that it could ruin your life," she says at one point. "I don't think that I ever would be." It is not simply an unhistorical reading that gives this line its resonance: this is a genuine *cri de coeur*. "You're trying to be something you're not," her father tells her when she "puts on airs." And his accusation is precisely true. But what, exactly, is she trying to be? The answer, overwhelmingly, is that she wants to transcend both her class and her sex. Her rebellion has large implications, which the text struggles to contain; the ultimate suppression of Queenie's sexuality, which is far more dangerous than Sam's or Reg's radicalism, becomes as well a suppression of her class disenchantment. Deserted by her lover in a foreign land, Queenie learns through suffering, is brought back to her old life by her faithful Bill, and slides imperceptibly into her role as wife and mother.

The film does not entirely contain the disturbance Queenie has introduced, in part because Kay Walsh's strong presence and her director-husband's sympathetic marshaling of that presence lends an urgency to Queenie's rebellion only sporadically evident in other parts of the film. Queenie is the first of a number of Lean characters, most of them women, whose primary characteristic is an unfocused but powerful yearning for something more, something different, something better. Like Laura Jesson and Madeleine Smith and Jane Hudson and Rosy Ryan, Queenie does not know her place, does not accept the role in which she finds herself. Walsh and Lean express this yearning with an intensity that threatens the integrity of Coward's text, calling into question all of its assumptions, but in particular the class assumptions that continuously inform it. If Queenie is reintegrated by the film's closure, she is so only schematically. Like Bob Mitchell's absent wife, she literally ceases to exist, at least as the person she was. But the repression has been so obvious and so thorough that her presence continues to resonate long after the film has ended.

Blithe Spirit (1945)

Few would argue that *Blithe Spirit*, either as a play or as a film, provides much more than a "frivolous, diverting, and inconsequential" experience, as George Perry summarizes Lean's third Noel Coward adaptation.[11] Lean perhaps saw the film more as a technical challenge than as an opportunity to speak in his own voice about matters that concerned him. Coward had constructed his "improbable farce in three acts" on a foundation of supernatural whimsy and theatrical hocus-pocus, and the major problem for Lean was how to translate these elements into a film without allowing the technical legerdemain to deflect attention from Coward's brittle discussion of love and marriage. In the course of solving technical problems, however, Lean slightly rearranges the emotional and psychological matrix Coward has provided. If *Blithe Spirit* is not yet a Lean film, it nevertheless exhibits sporadic signs of a growing independence.

Considered simply as an adaptation, *Blithe Spirit* is an assured work. Lean smoothly disguises the play's more overt theatrical aspects without entirely denying its stage origins. Coward's *Blithe Spirit*, like any well-made play, depends in part on a rhythmic cycle of logically self-contained scenes (there are seven of them) that build up to clever curtain lines, each of which creates a blackout effect. Lean constructs a somewhat different rhythm for the film. Though the overall dramatic structuring of Coward's play remains undisturbed, Lean's editing disguises the discontinuities of scenic construction. For the most part, Lean resorts to straightforwardly invisible editing for dialogue scenes, keeping the flow of conversation going while lending visual variety to scenes that could easily become static. At times, he takes a lengthy, continuous block of dialogue and rearranges it both spatially and temporally. Coward's act 2, scene 1—the long quarrel between Charles and Ruth—is restructured so that it takes place in different parts of the house over breakfast, lunch, tea, and dinner. The conversation continues logically unbroken, but time and space become discontinuous. Although Lean breaks no new ground here (see, for example, the brilliant breakfast sequence in Orson Welles's *Citizen Kane*), there is a fine appropriateness to this arrangement. The leisurely, banal lives of Coward's upper-class characters receive extra emphasis: all they do, it seems, is eat, drink, and quarrel. In solving a technical and aesthetic problem, Lean manages to sharpen a latent thematic point.

While Lean restructures the play in order to provide his film with its own cinematic rhythm, he also finds ways of stressing rather than diminishing Coward's theatrical tone and look. The drawing-room atmosphere is retained: though gestures are made in the direction of opening up the action by taking characters out of doors or to new locations, these are kept to a minimum. Furthermore, Lean's low-angled shots seem designed to make us feel as if we were sitting front-row center. The film's attractively stylized colors (pastel shades), decor, lighting effects, and, especially, performances contribute as well to a sense of a specifically theatrical artificiality. Only in Lean's handling of the supernatural do we feel a productive tension between theatrical and cinematic conventions.

Coward's play is a ghost story, but his ghosts are far from spiritual. For *Blithe Spirit* to make its point, we must feel that Elvira, the ghost of Charles Condomine's first wife, is as solid and earthy as the "live" characters. The supernatural must be kept as natural as possible. To this end, Lean uses the conventional cinematic tricks at his disposal (double exposure, for example) very sparingly. He creates an objective/subjective ghost by manipulating the strategies of point-of-view editing in conjunction with simple, stage-derived techniques. Like her stage counterpart, Lean's Elvira is painted green (actually, she is gray in the play) from top to toe, so we must accept the fact that, in Coward's words, "she is not quite of this world." Much of the play's humor arises from the inability of Charles's second wife, Ruth, to see or hear Elvira even though Charles sees and hears her perfectly well. When Elvira's ghost first appears, we see her in those shots where the point of view is clearly Charles's or is unspecified, but we do not see her in shots that are meant to represent Ruth's point of view. This simple technique, which merely requires that Kay Hammond be absent from some shots and present in others (her "presence" signified by framing and composition), is specifically cinematic in that it draws on the ordinary editing codes of the cinema and employs a vocabulary familiar, if only unconscously, to any movie audience.

Ironically, this method of making his ghost appear and disappear calls attention to otherwise innocuous editing and camera placement, and careful viewers will note that Lean's management of Elvira's presence and absence is not consistent from shot to shot. Of course, he does not have to be too consistent: one does not expect logical behavior from a ghost. More to the point, however, Lean can allow himself a certain amount of arbitrariness quite simply because, in seeming contradiction of what I have just written, point of view in the cinema is not as clear-cut, as readily understood a set of codes as it seems to be. The whole issue is highly problematical. When is a point-of-view shot not a point-of-view shot? In some shots, we see Charles talking with Elvira, who is visible. Such a shot, presumably, is *not* from Ruth's point of view, or Elvira would be invisible. We simply accept the seeming discrepancy here as we do in similar situations that do not involve ghosts in other films. The interesting thing here is that the discrepancies of editing add to our pleasure in a very specific way. Lean has taken advantage of the fact that in the cinema the camera, as Edward Branigan has shown, rather than having some profilmic life or meaning of its own, is simply "a construct of the spectator, a hypothesis *about space* . . . a label applied by the reader [viewer] to certain plastic transformations of space"[12] and not—or, at least, not consistently—the surrogate for any specific or consistent point of view.

Elvira, then, achieves ghostliness through a mixture of theatrical and cinematic effects. She is theatrical in the sense that her body remains (for the most part) substantial, her other-worldliness suggested through makeup and costuming; she is cinematic in the way she disappears from some shots and reappears in others. Occasionally she becomes a more conventional movie ghost. In one scene, for example, Ruth walks—surprisingly—right through Elvira, who is sitting at the bottom of the stairs. I say surprisingly because we are not constantly made aware of Elvira's permeability: much to our amusement, Elvira, too, is surprised. Whenever Lean does fall prey to the usual "Invisible Man" jokes, the film becomes unconvincing. The "invisible" Elvira driving a car, for example, is too hoary a cliché to be very funny: *Topper* (1937) did it better.

Despite his adroit handling of the supernatural, Lean directs *Blithe Spirit* in such a way as to tone down the whimsy and lightness of Coward's play. Just as he will work against the grain of romanticism in even his most romantic films, Lean here maintains a cool and critical distance from his characters. *Blithe Spirit*, as a result, emerges as a much more serious film than one would anticipate from a reading of Coward's play. On the stage, *Blithe Spirit* was an amusing, frequently misogynistic, exercise in witty

Margaret Rutherford (at window), Kay Hammond, and Rex Harrison in Blithe Spirit.

repartee; not, it must be said, Coward at his best. As Douglas McVay remarks, "the play's limitations of humour, springing from its limitations of humanity, are still apparent."[13] The convenient deaths of Charles's wives are wish-fulfillment fantasies, the implication being throughout that Charles much prefers to have Elvira around as a ghost than either wife in the flesh. The film seems far less sympathetic to Charles than does the play. Lean's direction of Rex Harrison stresses the passivity and coldness of Charles Condomine's character at the expense of his wit and presence of mind. Helpless and ineffectual, a virtual Ping-Pong ball for his wives, dead and alive, to play with, Charles fails to involve us very deeply in his problems (although my impression of Noel Coward's 1956 television appearance as Charles has dimmed, I seem to recall a far livelier, more self-consciously "comic" performance). Our sympathies, such as they are, are very much with the women; the play's misogyny becomes, in the film, Charles's misogyny. Both women—or all three, if we include Madame Arcati, played with magnificent dottiness by Margaret Rutherford—exhibit more strength of character than Charles and are thus more appealing. In particular, Kay Hammond's delicious vulgarity and eccentric sense of humor lend Elvira force and substance; even her strange delivery of lines, a sort of laconic slur, seems oddly right.

Ultimately, none of these characters engages us very deeply. Manny Farber, in a typically acerbic, negative review of the film in the *New Republic,* pointed at the truth without quite seeing its significance. "These people," he wrote, "seem to be stuffed with sawdust; their chief expressions are cruelty, boredom, sick amusement, distaste, limp superiority, fatigue, distrust; often they seem to be trying to laugh."[14] He both overstates the matter and fails to consider the extent to which this may be part of the film's meaning. As frothy and inconsequential as *Blithe Spirit* may be on the surface, we can sense, not very far beneath the brittle dialogue and lovely drawing rooms and smart clothes, a dark and rather unpleasant world. Without banishing the spirit of comedy or distorting Coward's intentions, Lean gives this darker side its due.

3

Lean's "Coming of Age": *Brief Encounter* (1945)

BRIEF ENCOUNTER may be among the most fondly remembered films of the 1940s. People who saw Lean's film when it was initially released retain for it a warm and sentimental affection: for many—particularly female—viewers, it seemed to present in a painfully poignant way a theme most contemporary movies treated as melodrama. The story of an "ordinary" married woman who falls in love with an "ordinary" married man, only to give him up and return to her husband and children, *Brief Encounter* reached profoundly into the core of an audience made weary by war and grimly facing an uncertain peace. But Lean's film is no period document, as some critics suggest, though it certainly documents its period. We cannot, of course, see the film today in quite the same way its original audience saw it: too much has happened, socially as well as cinematically, since then. Nevertheless, *Brief Encounter* remains an honest and moving expression of frustrated romance. It remains, as well, a virtuoso piece of filmmaking that marks David Lean's cinematic coming of age. Although the script is once again by Noel Coward, who also produced, Lean's independent contribution was for the first time generally recognized. *In Which We Serve*, *This Happy Breed*, and *Blithe Spirit* had been seen as Noel Coward films; *Brief Encounter* was a David Lean film.

Coward, Lean, and their collaborators fashioned *Brief Encounter* from Coward's one-act play "Still Life," which dramatizes the entire history of a love affair between two married people, Laura Jesson and Alec Harvey, who meet by chance, fall in love, and eventually decide to part forever, all within the refreshment area of the Milford Junction railway station. "Still Life" was one in a sequence of nine plays presented three at a time on three successive evenings under the general title *Tonight at Eight-Thirty* (1936). Taken as a group, these brief plays display—"show off" might be more accurate—Coward's versatility as playwright and, since he starred in all of them with Gertrude Lawrence, as actor as well. A mixture of the comic, the serious, and the musical, *Tonight at Eight-Thirty* for the most part features the witty and idle upper-class milieu with which Coward's work is primarily identified. Several of the plays, however, have middle-

Celia Johnson and Trevor Howard in Brief Encounter.

and lower-class themes, notably: "Red Peppers," "Fumed Oak," and "Still Life."

Because "Still Life" is a short play, Coward the screenwriter can retain in *Brief Encounter* virtually all of Coward the playwright's dialogue. Most adaptations require compression, but the challenge here was to expand the forty-five-minute play into a ninety-minute film. "Still Life" takes place entirely in the refreshment room of Milford Junction station; *Brief Encounter* ranges from Laura Jesson's home to the apartment of Alec's friend Stephen and takes us to restaurants, parks, train compartments, shops, a cinema, and so forth. As will be seen, this "opening out" is all to the good. The original play is perhaps too much a tour de force: an entire affair is somewhat implausibly presented over cups of tea and Banbury buns. Although ingeniously crafted, "Still Life" lacks emotional depth. The film allows us to see the relationship develop and grow whereas the play merely tells us about it. At the same time, the film covers a shorter period than the play. The love affair in "Still Life" develops over a year; *Brief Encounter* covers a mere six weeks. Laura and Alec meet, all told, seven times, including their initial, momentary encounter and a subsequent meeting where they see each other only long enough to say goodbye until the following week. Once again, this is an improvement, adding both poignancy and a sense of headlong abandon, of urgency, to the romance. The new time scheme also helps to cover another change, one required by the censor: in the play, Laura and Alec consummate their affair; in the film, they do not.

But the most important difference between play and film is that in the latter, Laura Jesson is the narrator. *Brief Encounter* consists primarily of flashbacks containing Laura's memories. This radical restructuring has several formal consequences. For one thing, the film seems more novelistic than theatrical in texture. For another, we now have a strong point of view with which to identify. Thematically, the meaning of Coward's story becomes radically transformed. Without any question, Laura Jesson's narration makes *Brief Encounter* a richer and more complex experience than it would be without it. There is a distance between the story and its presentation that allows us to view the narrative as pervasively subjective. Not that Laura remembers anything that did not happen; rather, her emotions and her imagination frequently color the events she recounts. Furthermore, she is not telling this story to any specific listener: she merely imagines that she is talking to her husband. Actually, she is talking to herself. Both the story's reticence and its romanticism are hers. *Brief Encounter* becomes a woman's story literally as well as thematically.

"I am a happily married woman," Laura says at the beginning of her internal narration, and though the phrase has an inevitably ironic ring to it (people who are happy do not need to say so, particularly to themselves), we believe that she means what she says. As marriages go, hers

Celia Johnson and Cyril Raymond in Brief Encounter.

seems to be a good one. Laura's house appears warm, her relationship with her husband spontaneous. Fred Jesson is in every way a decent fellow. All of this should point to a perversity in Laura's falling in love with another man. In a way, Laura does act perversely. We do not really notice this most of the time because the film makes her perversity seem not merely natural but inevitable. That Laura's affair has no obvious motivation makes her situation that much more poignant. Laura, like many of Lean's women, acts out of an implicit rebellion against the conditions of life itself, against the limitations of ordinary human existence, limitations that traditionally circumscribe women's lives much more radically than men's. I am not suggesting that the film is an especially feminist statement, but simply that Lean here reveals an instinctive understanding of the social and psychological forces that restrict the imaginative lives of women. All of this, it should be emphasized, is worked into the film's texture with remarkable economy. Little is said, but much is implied.

In nearly every way, *Brief Encounter* is Laura's story rather than Alec's; it is her crisis, her struggle. At the outset, Alec's motives might even seem suspect. It is he who "comes on" to her, forcing the issue at every point, keeping the relationship going. But to what end? The question is difficult to answer since we know next to nothing of what he feels and almost never see him away from the railway station or apart from Laura. Trevor Howard, who plays Alec with great charm, sincerity, and warmth, gives away very little of the inner man. There is, in a sense, no "objective" Alec at all: he is an idealized—but not too idealized—projection of Laura's romantic yearning. His boyish enthusiasm and social idealism provide an appealing contrast to her husband's stolid domesticity. Alec, we can guess from scattered clues, finds himself trapped in a passionless marriage: an affair, for him, fulfills an immediate and powerful need. He has less to lose, less need to count the consequences. With Laura, matters are far more complicated.

The complexities of Laura's situation in a large part express themselves through Celia Johnson's finely tempered performance. Johnson's screen persona hints at a strong element of repression lying beneath a patina of conventional niceness. In *This Happy Breed*, the practical, commonsensical woman she plays often seems on the very edge of a hysteria that can never find its way to the surface. In *Brief Encounter*, the cool brittleness of Laura Jesson's character is softened by the release of repressed passion. We are moved by Laura's experience in part because she is not—contrary to the way she presents herself—merely a "nice" person: she is, rather, a woman who has learned to cope, to bury frustration, bitterness, and longing in an endless round of daily routine and family responsibility. In the place of deep feelings, she has cultivated a strict sense of decency and rectitude and a surface pleasantness, qualities that, however admirable, hardly substitute for genuine warmth and unconsidered kindness. Romance allows Laura Jesson to relax some elements of her personality while others are given the chance to blossom. These shifting tensions occupy the film's thematic center.

The romance in *Brief Encounter*, though real enough, becomes heightened by the emotional needs and imaginative self-indulgence Laura invests in it. We might say that the difference between the imagination and the reality of Laura's affair is the difference between "Flames of Passion" and "Gentle Summer": the former is the title of the film Laura and Alec see at the Milford Cinema while the latter (as the screen-within-the-screen credits inform us) is the title of the novel on which the film is based. Like the (no doubt Hollywood) filmmakers of this epic, Laura imaginatively transforms a reticent, low-key encounter into a highly charged affair. At one point in the film, Laura reveals her fantasies. She sees herself and Alec in a variety of conventionally "glamorous" romantic situations: at the Paris opera, on a tropical beach by moonlight, in a Venetian gondola, on the deck of an ocean liner. As she fantasizes, her train arrives at the station. "And all the silly dreams disappeared," she comments, "and I got out at Ketchworth and gave up my ticket." Silly as they might be, Laura's dreams are shared by us all at one time or another. Nothing remotely like them happens in *Brief Encounter*; indeed, nothing much of an external nature happens at all. Laura's dreams are impossible, not because they could not literally come true (lovers have walked on tropical beaches) but because they merely symbolize a yearning to be someone else, to be other than what she is. A pleasant-looking doctor with ambitions for a career in preventive medicine hardly answers to her longings and imaginings: if he did, she would not need the fantasies he inspires; Milford Junction would be Venice enough.

The world Milford Junction represents in fact lies as far from Venice as one could imagine: Lean and his collaborators quite consciously create a mise-en-scène imbued with the everyday. It is, at the same time, a very artificial, very selective world. *Brief Encounter* may be a nearly perfect example of the closed film, a film in which, as Leo Braudy writes, "the world of the film is the only thing that exists."[1] Both thematically and materially, Lean's film is framed and contained both by its opening and closing shots and by the four straight lines that constitute the filmic image. The credit sequence provides a microcosm of the whole. A train moves from left to right as the credits begin; another moves from right to left as they end. During the credits, we hear a portion of Rachmaninoff's Second Piano Concerto. This is to be quite explicitly a film about meetings, arrivals, crossings, and departures: the movements of our everyday lives played out against powerful, frequently submerged emotions. The trains that start off the film serve both to define its world—Milford and Milford Junction station—and prefigure its theme. And Laura Jesson's narration, which implies a subjective, limited reality, further contains and delimits the filmic universe of *Brief Encounter*.

Lean specifically enforces narrative closure by depicting the lovers' final separation twice over, at the beginning and at the end of the film. The first time, before Laura's explicit narrative has begun, we are given only a vague impression of what is going on: the remainder of the film explains the meaning and significance of these first few moments. In repeating the scene, Lean employs different camera placements and editing patterns. We now see things we did not see before (Laura's near suicide attempt, for example), and we know things we did not know before. Alec's brief, furtive squeeze of Laura's shoulder intrigues us at the beginning of the film; when we see the same gesture at the end, its emotional force is that much more intense for the repetition. This framing device, which provides the film with something like the structure of a mystery story, intensifies the audience's awareness of the film as film, laying bare the narrative structure and making explicit the filmmakers' manipulation of narrative elements. The second time around, we not only think "we've seen this before" but also "we've been shown this before, but in a different way."

We also know, with some regret, that the film, like the affair, is nearly over. The narrative closes on itself: by beginning over again, the film signals its termination.

Complementing these specific forms of narrative enclosure, Lean's visual style evokes, within the context of a superficial realism, a highly selective, artificially arranged world. There are, for example, very few people in *Brief Encounter* who are not absolutely necessary to the plot. This may in part reflect the film's origin as a one-act play designed for a limited cast, but the effect, in any case, is to isolate and focus on Laura and Alec and their concern. In a number of scenes, they appear to exist in total isolation: Milford Junction station must be one of the most forlorn places in England. The film thus constructs an objective reflection of Laura's subjective vision. For her, there are times when she and Alec are the only people in the world. The art direction and cinematography contribute greatly to this sense of a self-enclosed world. The sets and locations have a tonal unity and an overall grayness that provide the film with a specific "look." Throughout, Lean maintains a tension between surface realism and stylization. The careful detailing of the decor is formalized by calculated camera angles and precise framing and editing.

Indeed, for all of the "matter-of-factness" of its theme and the ordinariness of its milieu ("it all started on an ordinary day, in the most ordinary place in the world"), *Brief Encounter* has a strong filigree of expressionism running through it. Our awareness of Laura Jesson's narrative as a specific, imaginative construct is frequently underlined by various formal cinematic techniques. At one point, for example, as Laura begins to lose herself in reverie, her surroundings darken and sounds fade out. In several shots, the transitions between Laura the narrator and Laura's narration are made by means of slow dissolves that result in an image of Laura watching herself. The famous tilted-camera sequence, externalizing Laura's state of mind as she contemplates suicide, provides another instance of extreme stylization. Lean breaks the surface of reality and forces us, in an almost Brechtian way, to stand back and consider what we see rather than simply becoming involved in it. Another highly expressionistic moment occurs soon after Laura has run away in shame and confusion from the interrupted tryst at the apartment of Alec's friend Stephen. The published script well describes the effect: "Dissolve to a shot of the war memorial. The foreground of the shot is composed of part of the war memorial statue: a soldier's hand gripping a bayoneted service rifle. Beyond it Laura is seen as a tiny figure walking towards a seat near the base of the memorial."[2] This highly formalized shot, insofar as it contains specific meanings, suggests that private life is overshadowed by public affairs and that Laura's problems are, in the larger scheme of things, relatively insignificant. More generally, the shot reflects Laura's state of mind, in which the war memorial becomes a looming witness to her sin and folly. Once again, Lean keeps us at a distance and asserts the values of reason while acknowledging the claims of emotion. It is this balance between emotion and reason, engagement and detachment, that accounts in large measure for the film's effectiveness. A sentimental, potentially lugubrious story is controlled by an objective, self-conscious cinematic style.

The use of Rachmaninoff's C-minor Concerto is probably the most brilliant example of the way the film creates an ongoing tension between realism and stylization. Interestingly, the music has been one of the most frequently criticized aspects of *Brief Encounter,* primarily because its function has been generally misunderstood. Rachmaninoff's highly charged piano concerto was not chosen to provide the film with a spurious romantic coloring the filmmakers were unable to summon up by other means. We must first note that the music is, ostensibly at least, diegetic: it emanates from the Jessons' radio and plays throughout the greater part of Laura's narrative reverie. Thus, we sometimes hear the music during a transition between the narration and the narrative frame (and vice versa). At other times, it seems to function as conventional background music, much in the manner of any film score. But even in those moments, it tends to remain rational, reminding us of Laura's status as narrator: the music is part of her consciousness, and we are thus made aware that her sensibility to some extent qualifies what we see and hear. For Laura, Rachmaninoff's music is an appropriate background to the story she is telling (even though, we should not forget, she did not consciously choose it; it just "happened" to be playing on the radio). For us, the effect is more complex. In some scenes, the music sweeps us along into Laura's consciousness, forcing us to share her emotions. In other scenes, the music adds a ludicrous dimension, underlining the gap between illusion and reality. Or both effects may coexist, contributing to an enrichment of the cinematic experience. When, for example, Alec tells Laura of his "special pigeon," preventive medicine, his enthusiastic recital of various kinds of coal dust is accompanied by the concerto's swelling strains. The comic effect depends on our awareness that we are sharing Laura's response to Alec. But the effect is not merely comic: we are equally compelled to realize the extent to which Laura can ignore commonplace reality in her yearning for a transcendent experience.[3]

The music serves another function as well. Rachmaninoff offers a sharp contrast to the other sounds by which Laura and Alec are constantly surrounded: the clatter of passing trains (sometimes so loud as to make conversation virtually impossible), the warning bells, and the steam whistles are all signs of both the precariousness and the peculiarly public nature of their romance. And then there is the music of the ladies' orchestra at the Kordomah Café; the movie theater organ; the melodramatic score for the trailer to "Flames of Passion"; the voices of Albert (north of England), Myrtle (pseudorefined), Dolly (irritatingly constant), Beryl (vulgar), Stephen (effete), and Fred (soothing and reasonable). This is a film in which sound is used self-consciously and with great subtlety. The place names themselves—Milford Junction, Ketchworth, Churley, Longdean, Perford—conspire against the lovers: it would be hard to imagine more chilling-sounding locales for the playing out of romantic agonies. The concerto allows Laura to drown out the other sounds, the everyday noises that threaten romance. But ordinary sounds cannot be drowned out; they, too, pervade Laura's consciousness and become a part of her secret, romantic world. The whistle of a train, heard as Laura talks with her husband, takes her mind back to Milford Junction and to Alec.

Sounds contribute only one element to the tension between romantic imaginings and a pervasively antiromantic atmosphere. Visually, *Brief Encounter* seems bathed in gray. "I believe we should all behave quite differently if we lived in a warm, sunny climate all the time," Laura says at one point. "We shouldn't be so withdrawn and shy and difficult." Laura, of course, gives voice to a conventional British sentiment. But Lean's mise-en-scène supports her viewpoint. Not only do a number of scenes take place at night, but even the daytime looks like February. Alec and Laura spend an afternoon on a lake where all the boats have been covered up for the winter. Even when Laura tells us that the day is lovely, we see bare trees and washed-out winter light. This is indeed a drab world, a world of stunted and repressed emotions.

Within the controlled, limited mise-en-scène the filmmakers have created for *Brief Encounter*, every detail of the fictive world becomes potentially charged with meaning. Most obviously, the trains that pass in and out of Milford Station reflect and intensify the film's plot and theme. Trains carry Laura and Alec toward and away from each other. Passing trains, though their noise frequently drowns out conversation between them, help to shut out the rest of the world while paradoxically reminding them of the world's existence. A cinder from a train blows into Laura's eye and brings Alec into her life. The speed, force, and noise of trains may represent passion (an express crashes through the station as the lovers kiss in the tunnel beneath), but these very qualities imbue them with malevolence as well: in despair, Laura contemplates throwing herself in front of one. Trains imitate the film's plot. They, too, are ships (as it were) that pass in the night, going in opposite directions on different tracks. On a more mundane level, trains are simply The World: time, work, responsibility, practicality; everything, in short, that works against romance.

It is not by chance that *Brief Encounter* begins with the stationmaster, Albert Godby (Stanley Holloway), expressing satisfaction that his trains are precisely on time. The world of Milford Junction is one of bells and clocks, of schedules, of regular arrivals and departures. Time and routine and habit provide the texture for Laura Jesson's life. Her Thursday trips to Milford, conceived as a break from the everyday, have developed a structure of their own. "I do the week's shopping, change my library book, have a little lunch, and generally go to the pictures," she explains to Alec. "Not a very exciting routine, really, but it makes a change." An affair, of course, can itself take on aspects of routine; illicit love requires a schedule. The film's own structure, so neatly and precisely determined, threatens to absorb the love affair into itself. As a result, we are almost relieved when Laura and Alec decide not to see each other again. However great and painful the loss, this is one part of their lives that will never ossify, never become merely another habit within a life of habit. The brief encounter between a man and a woman conventionally time-bound introduces a foreign element into the body of their lives; as such, it must be rejected. But, or so we are pleased to hope, it leaves its mark on both of them, remains always a sign of the irrational, the unexpected, the unplanned for.

In the 1940s, *Brief Encounter* was valued highly for its insistent "realism"—everyday people in an everyday setting; a poignant, downbeat denouement—and its quiet reticence. Perhaps in response to these very qualities, a reaction against the film has set in in recent years. Raymond Durgnat, in *A Mirror for England*, writes of his experience of the film at a 1965 revival:

> To see [*Brief Encounter*] again twenty years on . . . is to see another film entirely. Not that it no longer rings true. But the lovers in the drab Milford Junction buffet seem so strained, guilty, cowed, and therefore cold, that in 1965 the audience in this usually polite and certainly middle-class hall couldn't restrain its derision and repeatedly burst into angry exasperated laughter.[4]

One suspects Durgnat never saw the film for what it was in the first place. As I have already suggested, if *Brief Encounter* is not about people who are "withdrawn and shy and difficult" (as Laura describes herself), it is not about anything at all (which is one reason, among others, why a 1975 remake starring Richard Burton and Sophia Loren seemed so ludicrous). There are, undeniably, some false notes in Lean's film. The scenes with Albert and Myrtle, the stationmaster and café hostess whose flirtation provides a comic and earthly parallel to the restrained and anxious protagonists, counterpoints the main plot perhaps too schematically. The interrupted "tryst" at the flat of Alec's friend Stephen seems oddly handled. Why, one wonders, was it necessary to make Stephen, who unexpectedly walks in on Alec and Laura, so smarmy and effete? Lean and Coward, it seems to me, overemphasize the lovers' humiliation. These, however, are minor blemishes. A problem of somewhat greater moment, perhaps, lies in the script's pointed demonstration of just how "ordinary" and conventional Alec Harvey and (especially) Laura Jesson are; "ordinariness" threatens to become a necessary complement to middle-class life. Fortunately, Lean's tact and the credibility Celia Johnson and Trevor Howard bring to their roles virtually overcome the script's occasionally condescending tone.

The attitude of Durgnat's mid-1960s audience (and, to some extent, his own attitude as well) can perhaps best be explained by citing George Perry's comment on the film in *The Great British Picture Show.* "Today," Perry writes, "the couple would have been in bed at the first whistle, and that would have been that, but to students of the *mores* of an earlier generation it offers a fascinating insight into the collective psychology of its day."[5] Thus does Lean's film become a period piece. But this is altogether the wrong way to view not only *Brief Encounter* but "today" as well. The assumption that a respectable, middle-class woman of any time would as a matter of course commit casual adultery is in itself naive. One suspects that people who take such a line belong to an older generation, confused and shocked by their understanding of the "sexual revolution," a defective understanding that leads them to perceive the world as it is not. Perry's comments, it seems to me, will seem dated long before the film does (indeed, they are probably dated already). The film's characters behave very much as people in their position at any time or in any place would behave. Their doubts and hesitations, their pangs of conscience, and the exhilaration and simple pleasure they take in each other's company seem entirely human and entirely believable. The fact that they do not actually make physical love is beside the point. Perhaps Noel Coward should be given the last word on the subject. In the play—but not in the film—Alec says to Laura, "It's no use running away from the truth, darling—we're lovers, aren't we? If it happens or if it doesn't, we're lovers in our hearts."

Brief Encounter placed Lean among the world's premier film directors. In America, he became the first British director to be nominated for an Academy Award. Even British critics, usually restrained in their enthusiasm for the home product, began to take notice, and Lean was perceived as the new hope of British films. *Brief Encounter* was the kind of film critics could like. As John Ellis has pointed out, "The period of 1942–9 was one in which commercial production for the first time began to undertake a series of films which accorded with the critics' definition of 'quality.'"[6] "Quality," for these critics, meant restraint, good taste, humanist values, moral purpose, unobtrusive technique, and, most of all, "realism." From now on, all of Lean's films would be judged by a set of criteria distilled from these critics' understanding of *Brief Encounter.* This understanding, of course, was severely limited: the artfulness, the artificiality, of Lean's film was overlooked or undervalued. The success of *Brief Encounter*, although it must have been gratifying to him at the time, was something Lean would never quite live down.

4

Lean and Dickens

BETWEEN 1945 and 1950, one historian writes, "British films rose to an apogee, then fell to an apology."[1] For Lean, the apogee came when he ended his association with Noel Coward and turned to Charles Dickens with an adaptation of *Great Expectations* (1946), a film that was greeted with even more enthusiasm than *Brief Encounter* had been. Richard Winnington, writing in *Penguin Film Review*, called it "a landmark in the history of British Films" and hailed Lean as "Britain's leading film director."[2] In Hollywood, *Great Expectations* was recognized with Oscars for black and white photography, art direction, and set decoration; it was also nominated for best film, best direction, and best adaptation. Given this success, *Oliver Twist* (1948), his second Dickens adaptation, was bound to disappoint the critics. Winnington felt that Lean had "failed for the first time . . . to move forward with a new film."[3] Today, the differences between these films seem as striking as their similarities. The earlier film follows Dickens with more fidelity, particularly in structure and plot, than the later one and tells a more compelling story—one of the world's great stories. But *Oliver Twist*, in part because it does not adhere as closely to its source, may be the more interesting film. Each film, in any event, has its own distinctive style, and each finds, through that style, meanings parallel to but not identical with Dickens's meanings.

Great Expectations (1946)

In chapter 14 of Charles Dickens's *Great Expectations*, Pip, the protagonist/narrator, pauses in his story to give voice to a profound sense of dissatisfaction: "What I wanted, who can say? How can *I* say, when I never knew?"[4] Although these words are not repeated in the film, they might easily serve as an epigraph not only for Pip but for other of Lean's protagonists as well, from Queenie Gibbons in *This Happy Breed* to Rosy Ryan in *Ryan's Daughter*. The theme recurs in *Madeleine* and *Lawrence of Arabia*, in *The Passionate Friends* and *Summer Madness*, in *Brief Encounter*

Top: Martita Hunt as Miss Havisham and Anthony Wager as the young Pip in Great Expectations. *Bottom: Finlay Currie as Magwich in* Great Expectations.

and *Doctor Zhivago.* His choice of *Great Expectations* as his first film independent of Noel Coward was thus perhaps not as arbitrary as he and others have made it sound. Pip, who longs for status and for money and, having achieved both, finds they are as ashes in his mouth, combines in himself the romantic longings of Lean's female and the obsessive behavior of his male protagonists. In form, too, *Great Expectations* fits Lean's propensity for subjective, retrospective narratives, stories where the consciousness of the narrator and the way the narrative unfolds become as important as the story itself.

Lean's version of *Great Expectations* captures with remarkable fidelity the tone, mood, characters, and themes of Charles Dickens's great work. Regarded simply as an adaptation, it succeeds as have very few other attempts to bring Dickens to the screen. In part, this can be attributed to characteristics of the novel itself, which is more tightly plotted and less ornamented than many of Dickens's tales. By the time he came to write *Great Expectations,* a masterpiece of his maturity, Dickens had, in the words of K. J. Fielding, "completely mastered the skill of construction."[5] Lean adheres to the novel's structure, giving the illusion, which only a rereading of the novel can dispel, of including virtually everything. Actually he could not and did not reproduce the entire novel on film. But what literary editing he and Ronald Neame did was more a matter of judicious, if wholesale, pruning than of slashing or cutting. Of Dickens's fifty-nine chapters, the film retains at least some part of forty-four. Furthermore, all of the major characters, and most of the minor ones, make some appearance in the film. The changes and alterations do not seriously dilute the coherence of Dickens's plot, a plot that, taken in itself, has mythic resonances of extraordinary power.

Lean's first task, then, was to preserve the essential contours of Dickens's tale. The greater challenge, however, was to evoke the novel's spirit and style, a challenge he meets to a remarkable degree. The voice-over narration preserves at least a suggestion of a first-person point of view and retains the flavor of Dickens's own voice, at the same time providing transitional and summary bridges. Furthermore, Lean chose to reproduce, as much as possible, the novel's dialogue, sometimes word for word. This may seem an obvious enough choice, but it requires an awareness of and a faith in the dramatic potential of Dickens's prose that other adaptors of Dickens have not always exhibited. What Lean realized is that in Dickens, perhaps more than in any other English novelist, characters live in the way they speak. The language of Dickens, his distinctly rhetorical style, his patterning and repetitions, his tricks of speech, may be what is most distinctive in his novels. By preserving even a small percentage of this linguistic texture, Lean captures what we experience as the inescapably Dickensian atmosphere.

For the most part, however, the language, the words, must be translated into images, into what we see on the screen. Characters, of course, are situated at that point where language shades off into, becomes, image. Here, once again, Lean puts his faith in Dickens, and like him projects humanity's essential eccentricities without falling completely into caricature. Other film adaptations of Dickens either make the mistake of naturalizing his characters, turning them into more or less "ordinary" people (*Great Expectations*, USA, 1934; *Oliver Twist*, USA, 1933) or allowing the eccentricities to take over entirely (some of the characters in George Cukor's *David Copperfield* [1935] and Cavalcanti's *Nicholas Nickelby* [1946]; both are, however, quite good films). Interestingly, insofar as some of Dickens's characters are "flat" in E. M. Forster's usage of the term, they can be "rounded out" through judicious casting. To that end, Lean has filled even the smallest role with great care. A minor character like the "Aged Parent," who in the novel is little more than the sum of his eccentricities, and who appears only once in the film, gains considerably from the kind face and gentle manner of O. B. Clarence; occupying but a few moments of screen time, he is nonetheless memorable. Lean's Mrs. Joe, Wemmick, and Uncle Pumblechook, too, retain the flavor and quirky liveliness of their literary originals even though the film reduces their function and scope.

Lean's fidelity to Dickens transcends merely reproducing words and images from the novel, however. For the most part, this fidelity is illusion, sleight of hand. In actuality none (or almost none) of Dickens's novel is "in" the film at all. Even the dialogue taken directly from Dickens is, in the novel, words printed on a page whereas in the film they are mechanically reproduced sounds, which is not the same thing. Dickens's novel is present in the film *in reality* only at those very rare times when written words are literally reproduced either in the extradiegetic form of superimposed titles or in the form of signs, posters, etc., within the diegesis. In short, of the five cinematic codes identified by Christian Metz (the visual image, the musical sound, the verbal sounds of speech, sound effects, and the graphic form of the credits),[6] only one, the graphic form of words, can be transposed from a literary to a film text. This would be a point hardly worth making were it not that many discussions of film adaptation ignore the incontrovertible fact that the texture of a literary work can never truly be present in a film. A novel, as Roland Barthes shows, is a system of meaning, a "code of representation," whereas a film belongs to the order of the operable, "a code of execution."[7] A film, in the act of re-creating it, inevitably destroys a literary text. All that we can assert is that characters, settings, and plot are alluded to, more or less closely, when transferred from novel to film. At most, Lean's film is a free translation, a loose paraphrase, of Dickens's book.

Even the famous opening sequence, which seems so like our experience of the novel, achieves its effect in a manner very different from it. Here, with some minor ellipses, is the relevant passage from *Great Expectations*:

> Ours was the marsh country, down by the river, within, as the river wound, twenty miles of the sea. My first most vivid and broad impression of the identity of things, seems to me to have been gained on a memorable raw afternoon towards evening. At such a time I found out for certain, that this bleak place overgrown with nettles was the churchyard; and that Philip Pirrip, late of this parish, and also Georgiana wife of the above, were dead and buried; . . . and that the dark flat wilderness beyond the churchyard, intersected with dykes and mounds and gates, with scattered cattle feeding on it, was the marshes; and that the low leaden line beyond was the river; and that the distant savage lair from which the wind was rushing, was the sea; and that the small bundle of shivers growing afraid of it all and beginning to cry was Pip.
>
> "Hold your noise!" cried a terrible voice, as a man started up from among the graves at the side of the church porch. "Keep still, you little devil, or I'll cut your throat."[8]

One notes that Dickens, characteristically, gives the effect of simultaneity to what is necessarily a sequential description, primarily by employing a series of clauses all beginning with the connective "and" and separated by semicolons. His style is pictorial; in a sense, proto-cinematic.

The film parallels the Dickens passage quoted above via a sequence of eight shots.[9] The first, an extreme long shot, is of the Thames estuary at sunset. We see the very small image of a boy running right to left along the estuary bank; the sky is streaked with waning sunlight and stippled clouds; the camera tracks and pans with the boy, already identified as Pip, as he turns toward the camera, passes a gibbet at frame right, and then disappears off frame. In this first shot, twenty-five seconds of screen time, Lean presents us with Pip, with the marshes, and with the threat of death by hanging. The gibbet, it will be noted, is not mentioned in the quoted passage. Lean has simply picked up this detail from later in the chapter. In the second shot, Pip enters the churchyard (a studio set), carrying a bunch of holly. The atmosphere is threatening and eerie; the gravestones are unnaturally large and placed at odd angles; a crooked tree branch dominates the top half of the frame; the wind, its sound amplified and ominously distorted, whistles through the trees. Shots three and four depict Pip kneeling at his parents' grave; the wind becomes louder and Pip looks nervously over his shoulder toward the camera. Shot five is a point-of-view (POV) shot of the leafless branches of a tree. In shot six, Pip looks off in another direction and shot seven shows us what he is looking at: a ghostly, almost anthropomorphic tree. In shot eight, Pip jumps to his feet and runs from right to left, looking behind him as he runs. The camera pans with him and stops just as he bumps into the indefinite but threatening figure of a man (who does not, as at least one description of the sequence asserts, jump or pounce at Pip, though that is the impression one gets). The next shot is a close-up of Pip as he screams.

In discussing this sequence, the film's editor, Jack Harris, notes that "the difficulty in the editing was to decide on the exact frame up to which to leave the panning shot on the screen and to cut to the boy screaming. The effect aimed at was to leave the shot on the screen sufficiently long to let the audience see that the boy had run into a man—and not a very nice man, at that—but not sufficiently long to get a good look and be able to decide that he was after all something recognisably human."[10] Dickens achieved his surprise effect through the transition from one paragraph to the next: he employs the white space, the break in typography between the end of one sentence and the beginning of another to set up and punctuate his surprise. In translating Dickens's novelistic effect into specifically filmic terms, an equivalent was found for that paragraph break, which in itself could not be reproduced on film.

We can also see that Lean's sequence is both more and less rich than the Dickens passage: less rich because it omits the evocative precision of such phrases as "low leaden line," "distant savage lair," and "small bundle of shivers"; more rich because it includes, summarizes, makes "operable," much of the atmospheric suggestiveness of the first five or so chapters of the novel. It is in part this ability to summarize, to include in a single shot or in the transition from shot to shot what it would take the novelist pages to evoke, that allows a two-hour film any chance of rendering at all convincingly a five-hundred-page novel. Narrative and description are supplanted by the concreteness, the "thingness," of deliberately composed, lit, and photographed images that move—in short, by the cinema.

The sequence just described is the first of several that are quite purposely "bracketed," that stand as clearly marked pools in the film stream. At key moments in Pip's moral development, Lean creates striking, self-contained set-pieces that summarize some of the film's scattered thematic strands and mark the climax of a sustained narrative movement. The pervasive mysteriousness of Dickens's tale, for example, finds ideal expression in the pursuit of the convicts over the marshes. The images here are strikingly etched: a line of soldiers silhouetted against the darkening sky as Pip and Joe, also silhouetted, appear in the foreground; the hunting party crossing the graveyard; the two convicts, eerily captured in the stream of bright, harsh moonlight, wrestling clumsily on the mudflats; soldiers stumbling through the mud to seize their prey. Here, studio sets and studio lighting combine unapologetically with exterior locations and day-for-night photography to create a nightmarish, irrational world that will forever imprint itself on a boy's memory. Equally notable are such sequences as the return of Magwitch, introduced by a shot of rain-swept

London rooftops and textured by a patterned alternation of light and shade and high and low camera angles, and the fire at Satis House, where Lean's editing creates tension and drama while revealing, in such moments as when Pip pulls off the rotting cloth from the long banqueting table, the final crumbling away of Pip's foolish dream.

The strong visual style evident in these sequences and indeed at nearly every moment in the film owes its inspiration to a complex of sources and influences. Apart from the novel's specific verbal descriptions, a significant, indirect influence on the design and costuming of *Great Expectations* was Dickens's illustrators. Here, Lean and his collaborators were not as fortunate as they would later be with *Oliver Twist,* where they had the great George Cruikshank drawings to guide them. *Great Expectations* is one of those rare Dickens novels to appear without illustrations in its serial form. For its later publication in book form, a number of drawings were commissioned from Marcus Stone, one of the most pedestrian and conventional of Dickens's illustrators. His woodcuts contribute little to the look of the film. Instead, John Bryan and Wilfred Shingleton, the film's production designer and art director, respectively, probably depended on Hablot K. Browne (Phiz), Dickens's principal illustrator, and, to a lesser extent, on Cruikshank. Both of these artists were caricaturists, and thus well suited to Dickens's style. It is particularly in the set design that one detects Browne's influence: his drawing of Tom's-All-Alone for *Bleak House,* for example, must have inspired some of the London views in Lean's film. And both Browne and Cruikshank contribute greatly to the appearance of the more eccentric of the cast of characters. But the film's debt to them, though pervasive, is quite unspecific.

The sequences involving Miss Havisham exhibit a visual eclecticism. Although Satis House and its inhabitants are rendered in a manner true enough to the spirit of Dickens's text, the set design and decoration, the lighting, and the cinematography generally suggest the atmospherics of a horror film: dark nooks and crannies; low-key illumination; cobweb-covered objects; elaborately carved furniture; ever-present bric-a-brac. At the same time, Pip's entry into Satis House has an *Alice in Wonderland* quality to it. Pip is a small creature in an unrealistically large world (an effect achieved, to some degree, by the employment of a wide-angle, 24mm lens), smaller, even, than Estella, who is supposed to be about his age. This effect is emphasized in a shot of Pip framed by an archway in the background, pausing at the threshold of the house, while Estella waits for him in the foreground, as luminous and imposing as he is dark and unimpressive. Estella, in her frilly dress and shoulder-length hair, clearly a lovely young woman made to look like a child, is herself very Alice-like as Tenniel has drawn her. And Miss Havisham, with her peremptory manner, has much of the Queen of Hearts (the Queen of Broken Hearts?) about her. Seeing her from Pip's point of view, we would not be surprised to hear her say, "Off with his head." Whether or not Lewis Carroll and Sir John Tenniel had any direct influence on the filmmakers, the fairy-tale atmosphere, the evocation of a fantasy world, is certainly present in a concrete, detailed, pictorial manner. The film convincingly projects Pip's fantastic experience at Miss Havisham's strange, fearful, enchanted house.

Although the atmosphere, the Dickensian mood of *Great Expectations* owes much to Lean's concern for the purely graphic elements—photography, art direction, lighting, composition—his expert handling of the actors contributes nearly as much to the film's success. His choice of Anthony Wager to play Pip as a boy was close to ideal: attractive but not "pretty," pleasant but not sentimentalized, gentle and yet touched with a streak of pride that prepares us for the adult transformation, Wager provides Pip with strength and substance. John Mills has some initial difficulty making the transition to the adult Pip, looking rather too callow and foolish in his early scenes, but becoming more sure of himself once the transition has been accomplished. Playing against the grain of his pleasant image, he adopts a convincingly priggish, stiff-backed manner for his "gentleman" phase, later relaxing into the fully adult, gentle Pip of the last quarter of the film. As the young Estella, Jean Simmons is nearly perfect: coolly beautiful, saucy, cruel, sexually self-aware, she knowingly combines womanly elegance with girlish perversity. Lean has been criticized for having Estella look so much older than Pip, but Dickens allows for the disparity, Pip telling us that, although about his own age, Estella "seemed much older than I, of course, being a girl, and beautiful and self-possessed; and she was as scornful of me as if she had been one-and-twenty, and a queen." Inevitably, the adult Estella, as portrayed by Valerie Hobson, disappoints, and one feels that Jean Simmons (who was then seventeen) should, and easily could, have continued in the role.

Among the other major performers, Bernard Miles (Joe), Francis L. Sullivan (Jaggers), and Martita Hunt (Miss Havisham) all hold to the fine line between caricature and character. And Alec Guinness, as Herbert Pocket (a role he had played in his own stage adaptation of the novel), draws a whole inner life from a relatively minor character, his tentative, childlike manner and gentle simplicity precisely fulfilling Dickens's conception. But perhaps the most fully realized, truly moving characterization in the film is Finlay Currie as Magwitch. A large, ugly, and yet dignified figure, Currie's Magwitch, from his initial appearance in the graveyard to the moment of his death, manages to project both his literal function as one of society's outcasts and his symbolic role as Pip's fairy godfather. Currie interacts particularly well with Anthony Wager, responding to Pip's kindness and concern ("I'm glad you enjoy it, sir") with a mixture of gruffness, surprise, and pleasure that subtly hints at a continuing relationship. When Magwitch reappears years later, the odd delight he takes in having made Pip a gentleman is movingly palpable. The effect of Currie's very appearance—bull-head, hawklike nose, close-set eyes, clumsy body—illustrates the power of the cinematic image: Dickens never tells us precisely what his convict looks like, but to anyone who has seen Lean's film, Magwitch will forever bear the features of Finlay Currie.

If Lean's atmospherics and the characterizations provided by his actors are elements of *Great Expectations* generally praised both by contemporary reviewers and by later critics, his ending for the film has found far less favor.[11] The problem, however, is one he inherited. Dickens wrote two endings to *Great Expectations.* In his original, suppressed ending, Pip and Estella meet by chance on a London street a number of years after the main events of the novel, speak briefly, and part once again, presumably forever. In the published ending, Pip and Estella meet at the site of Satis House, realize their mutual love, and Dickens leaves us with the suggestion that they will now live happily ever after. For a long time, the original ending was considered the superior one, but in recent years critical favor has to some extent come around to the published version. Lean, for his part, creates a third version, close in spirit to but different in effect from the so-called "happy" ending. Only a short time after the death of Magwitch, Pip revisits Satis House. Visually and aurally, the film echoes Pip's first visit: links with the past are signaled by lighting, camera angles, and composition, and we also hear the ghostly voices of Pip, Estella, and Miss Havisham. Pip discovers Estella in the chair Miss Havisham used to occupy, and we see that she is lit and framed as Miss Havisham had been. The film here becomes a ghost story, a fairy tale, and Pip, like a fairy-tale hero, breaks the evil spell and rescues the princess. After tearing down the draperies to let in the sun ("I have come back, Miss Havisham—I have come back to let in the light"), he takes Estella by the hand and leads her out of the dungeon that threatened to imprison her.

Whatever our response to Lean's ending, it undeniably owes much to several explicit and implicit formulations provided by the novel itself. Perhaps perversely, Lean draws upon a passage from the novel that, in context, is pregnant with irony. At the beginning of chapter 29, Pip, sometime before he has discovered the truth of his inheritance, muses over Miss Havisham's motives as he prepares to pay her a visit.

> She had adopted Estella, she had as good as adopted me, and it could not fail to be her intention to bring us together. She reserved it for me to restore the desolate house, admit the sunshine into the dark rooms, set the clocks a going and the cold hearths a blazing, tear down the cobwebs, destroy the vermin—in short, do all the shining deeds of the young Knight of romance, and marry the Princess.[12]

All of this, of course, is precisely what does not happen in the novel, at least not literally, especially as Dickens first conceived his ending. And yet, Pip does win his princess in the published version, so that in effect if not in manner his daydream is fulfilled. Lean, in constructing his ending, realizes one of Dickens's major motifs. Dorothy Van Ghent, commenting on the novel, has observed:

> In the sense that one implies the other, the glittering frosty girl Estella, and the decayed and false old woman, Miss Havisham, are not two characters but a single one, or a single essence with dual aspects, as if composed by montage—a spiritual continuum, so to speak.[13]

The film makes the identification explicit, executing Dickens's intention, giving concrete form to abstract concepts.

In the end, then, Pip manages to win Estella and, presumably, her money as well. The film's major thrust, however, is not to reward Pip but to punish him for his class aspirations. The ending is, like the novel's in either version, precipitate and curtailed; the compression of time places the emotional emphasis more on the death of Magwitch than on the rebirth of Estella. Pip's winning of Estella, with or without the money, is meant to be the only meaningful reward—an uncertain one, given Estella's character. Love, family, home: these, the film implies, are the genuine values to which we should aspire. The hope of rising on the social ladder must be revealed as a chimera. In the film, though not in the novel, Bentley Drummle refuses to marry Estella once he discovers that her father was a convict. We are the class of our birth, not of our rearing.

It is perhaps not entirely coincidental that a film so concerned with class aspirations should have appeared at the very moment England was coming to terms with socialism. The Labour landslide of July 1945 sent nervous tremors throughout the upper and middle classes ("*we* are the masters now," one Labourite declared on election night). Regarded in this context, Lean's film becomes a middle-class parable for all who may be harboring "great expectations" of their own. For his part, Dickens was not as concerned with the class issue as he was with the movement of Pip's heart. In his novels, and particularly in *Great Expectations*, the creation of and solution to social problems are nearly always a matter of individual choice. The film, perhaps inevitably, simplifies Pip's psychology and to that extent places the matter of social status in the foreground. In a class-bound and therefore class-conscious society, aspirations to a higher sphere can be discouraged in two ways primarily. One is to suggest that either it cannot be accomplished at all or that it cannot be accomplished without simultaneously sacrificing all that is truly to be valued in oneself; the other way is to show that the object of desire is in fact worthless. In the novel, Pip becomes a snob before he becomes a gentleman: it is primarily Estella (who embodies something inherent in Pip's nature), not London friends and ready money, who makes him ashamed of Joe and the forge. In the film, however, only when Pip has become a gentleman does he become a snob. Bentley Drummle, in the novel, is a more or less uniquely boorish individual; in the film, his boorishness seems to consist entirely in being a gentleman. To be a gentleman, in short, is to be a prig, a bully, a stuffed shirt, an idler. Not only is gentleman status achieved at a terrible price, but it is not much of a goal in the first place. Lean's *Great Expectations,* frequently praised as a fine adaptation of Dickens while simultaneously deplored as escapism, may not be as irrelevant to postwar British society as some have found it.[14]

Oliver Twist (1948)

Clouds gather in a darkening sky; a leaf falls from the nearly bare branch of a skeletal tree; the wind lightly disturbs the still waters of a pond; another, even more withered tree branch sways in the breeze. Over the edge of a distant rise, a small, indistinct figure appears; on closer inspection we see a lovely young woman, pregnant and in obvious pain; ahead of her, the road stretches away; she pauses and peers into the darkness; exhausted, she walks on. A full moon, surrounded by dark clouds, illuminates the heavens; a cloud's threatening shadow passes over the lone traveler; lightning flashes; thorned branches sway in the wind; the young woman's face distorts with pain. In the distance, first a light and then a group of buildings emerge from the darkness; the woman's pain and her determination both intensify; lightning and rain; the woman quickens her step.

We see the dark branch of a prickly briar buffeted to and fro by the storm; the woman walks on; raindrops cover the surface of the pond; nearly faint, the mother-to-be hugs a signpost to steady herself. The distant buildings become more clearly discernible; the woman continues her journey. From behind an iron fence and in the light of a swinging, creaking lantern, we see her approach. She stands outside the gate, which someone proceeds to open as lightning illuminates the sign above: "Parish Workhouse." Time passes, the moon emerges from behind the clouds, and we hear the cry of an infant. The new mother, sickly and pale, lies on a crude wooden bed, her infant, wrapped in blankets, on the floor beside her.

The opening sequence graphically establishes the predominant style and mood of David Lean's *Oliver Twist:* a gothic atmosphere, evocative more of the Brontë sisters than of Dickens, and a situation that is the stuff of melodrama. Specifically, we are reminded of the silent film. No dialogue accompanies the first three and a half minutes of screen time; only sound effects complement the sequence of images. Lean's editing constructs a rhythm of contrasts: image and sound; narrative and picturesque; literal and symbolic; human and nonhuman; objective and subjective; realism and expressionism; dark and light; stillness and movement; birth and death. If the literary allusion is to the English Gothic, the cinematic allusions are to D. W. Griffith (*Way Down East; Orphans in the Storm*), to Russian montage, to German Expressionism. A complex circle of references closes here: as Griffith was influenced by Dickens and in turn influenced the Russian filmmakers Sergei Eisenstein and V. I. Pudovkin, so Lean, in translating Dickens, pays homage to Griffith and Soviet montage as well as to the German silent film. Eisenstein, in a now classic essay, "Dickens, Griffith, and the Film Today,"[15] traced some of these influences, and at the same time belittled the German achievement, embraced Griffith, and demonstrated that in his own films he had absorbed and pressed beyond these precursors. Though Lean is unlikely to have known of Eisenstein's 1944 essay (to which we shall return) before an English translation appeared in 1949, his film of *Oliver Twist* points, as had Eisenstein, to the subtle, complex, and dynamic interchange between the world of the verbal and the world of the visual.

Lean notably begins *Oliver Twist* with a prologue that has no direct progenitor in Dickens. Though some allusion is made to the travails Oliver's mother must have endured in the days before her labor, nothing in the novel precisely parallels the film's first sequence. Lean goes out of his way to establish a nonliterary narrative structure by avoiding voice-over narration, the opening of a book (both used in *Great Expectations*), words on the screen, or any of the other conventional devices that signify the film adaptation of a classic novel. It is only at the end of the "birth of Oliver" sequence that superimposed words appear on the screen and a voice intones: "Oliver cried lustily. If he could have known that he was an orphan, left to the tender mercies of the beadle and the matron, perhaps he would have cried the louder," a slight variant of the paragraph that closes Dickens's first chapter. If the film's opening sequence declares a flamboyantly "cinematic" independence from the novel (cinematic in the limited sense of employing self-consciously codes of lighting, editing, camera movement, framing, etc., that are generally associated with film), the remainder of the film does not entirely bear out the expectations raised; or, rather, it bears them out in unsuspected ways. For though Lean may begin by denying the novel, he is careful to create throughout the illusion of fidelity, an illusion that obscures the large transformation Dickens's text undergoes in the hands of Lean and his collaborators.

In reconstructing *Oliver Twist* for the screen, Lean and co-scriptwriter Stanley Haynes eliminated virtually half of the novel. Theirs, however, was a systematic, not a haphazard, editorial decision. Of Dickens's fifty-three chapters, the film draws substantially on the following: 1–2; 4–16; 20; 24; 26; 37–40; 45–48; 50. Lean ignores, in their entirety, chapters 3, 18, 21–22, 25, 27–36, 41–43, and 52–53. A remaining six chapters (17, 19,

23–24, 49, and 51) contain some lines of dialogue, some slight detail of characterization or plot that find their way into the film. If this last group is combined with the eliminated chapters, it will be seen that twenty-six chapters contribute little or nothing to the film, whereas twenty-seven chapters have been absorbed, to a greater or lesser extent, into the film-text. This breakdown of course ignores such matters as combined characters (e.g., Mrs. Mann and Mrs. Corney), substituted characters (Mr. Brownlow "takes over" some of the now absent Rose Maylie's functions; the Artful Dodger, not Noah Claypole, spies on Nancy), and transposed sequences (in the film, Nancy goes to the police station to check up on Oliver while the latter is still in custody, not, as in the novel, afterwards). I am also ignoring, for the moment, details of the film that have no precise original in the novel (most notably, Oliver's presence on the roof with Bill Sikes). In addition, one might adduce changes in setting (Monks and Fagin, in the film, confer at the Three Cripples, not at a secret hideout) as well as alterations in the temporal location of an object, place, or character.

Speaking quite generally and always keeping in mind that *Oliver Twist* as a film has a reality entirely independent of Charles Dickens's novel, we can suggest that Lean and his collaborators have heightened and reimagined the melodramatic aspects of the novel while eliminating some of the sentimentality and underplaying the role of coincidence and "providence" central to the novel's structure and theme. The film's climax, which places Oliver on the rooftops at the mercy of a desperate Bill Sikes, may be the most notable added melodramatic device. By thus putting Oliver in danger, the filmmakers of necessity save him from the highly unlikely circumstance of twice escaping his tormentors and twice ending up, purely by chance, in benevolent households, one of which is occupied by his father's oldest friend and the other by his mother's sister. The loss of the entire Rose Maylie episode can hardly be lamented by even the most fervent Dickens admirers.

Here, at least, the film—dare it be said—improves on Dickens's plot. For reasons not readily fathomed, Dickens separates Oliver entirely from Fagin and company precisely halfway through the novel (I am consulting an edition in which the text runs from page 23 to page 481; Oliver is dropped into a ditch by Bill Sikes on page 250; aside from a momentary, dreamlike glimpse, he does not see Fagin again until he visits him in prison in the novel's penultimate chapter). We do not return to Fagin, Bill Sikes, and Nancy for nearly a hundred pages, during the course of which we are introduced to a new set of remarkably uninteresting characters. After that, the novel more or less alternates between the Oliver plot and the Fagin/Sikes/Nancy plot. The only genuine suspense concerning Oliver in the second half of the novel involves the discovery of his parentage and the extent of his fortune. In short, the novel transfers its concern for Oliver's physical and moral well-being to a concern for class and money. Commenting on chapters 29 to 39 (a section omitted by Lean), Arnold Kettle writes:

> The basic conflict of the novel is brought, in this quarter, almost to a standstill; the people who have captured our imagination scarcely appear at all . . . we are not interested in the affairs of Rose and Harry Maylie; we do not care who Oliver's father was and, though we sympathise with Oliver's struggles, we do not mind whether or not he gets his fortune. . . . What engages our sympathy is not Oliver's feeling for the mother he never saw, but his struggle against his oppressors of which the famous gruel scene is indeed a central and adequate symbol.[16]

The film, by contrast, maintains an emphasis throughout on Oliver and the forces that threaten his destruction. The melodramatic texture that informs much of the novel becomes the film's primary formal organization. Dickens, perhaps because he identified strongly with his protagonist, did not wish to keep Oliver in constant danger and degradation. The second half of the novel thus compensates Oliver for the first half; the world of nightmare becomes the world of wish-fulfillment fantasy. Lean's film, on the other hand, projects an almost constant atmosphere of fear and danger interrupted only briefly by the idyll at Mr. Brownlow's house. Although the film tones down some of the novel's grimmer aspects—Fagin is less sinister, Bumble less brutal, Bill Sikes perhaps somewhat less explosive—its structure puts an enlarged emphasis on Oliver's workhouse experience. (It is surprising to discover, upon rereading the novel, that Oliver is out of the workhouse by chapter 4.) The film's narrative, then, is simple enough. Oliver escapes from one false family into another false family, briefly finds refuge with a "true" family, falls once again into the hands of the false family, and, finally, having in a sense helped to kill the false family, is reunited with his true family. Throughout, Oliver is a threatened child, a boy in distress, whose virtue and life both are at the mercy of sinister forces beyond his control. In short, Oliver Twist functions as the heroine does in traditional melodrama.

The melodramatic texture of Lean's *Oliver Twist* is at least as much a matter of its visual style as it is of its narrative structure. As has been noted a number of times, and as Lean himself asserted, *Oliver Twist* finds inspiration not only in Dickens's text but also in George Cruikshank's famous illustrations, illustrations so striking that they have developed a life nearly independent of the text they accompany. Indeed, when we say that Lean's film is remarkably "Dickensian" in flavor, we are quite as likely thinking of the visual world of Dickens's various illustrators as of the verbal world of his text. Cruikshank, in fact, is only one of the sources influencing the visual style of Lean's *Oliver Twist*, and his contribution, though crucial, is of a specific and limited nature. Some of his drawings provide a direct model for the mise-en-scène of particular sequences in Lean's film. The plate entitled "Oliver plucks up a Spirit," for example, influenced the set design, lighting, composition, and staging of the Oliver/Noah Claypole scenes in the Sowerberry kitchen. The film closely imitates the dynamic composition, the busy texture, the heavily filled space, the enclosed design, and the images of lanky Noah and blowsy Charlotte. Cruikshank's plate "The Meeting" (Rose Maylie, Mr. Brownlow, Nancy, and Noah Claypole in the shadows of London bridge), too, strongly influenced John Bryan's set design and Guy Green's lighting of the equivalent scene in the film. Similarly, the low-ceilinged, dark-cornered, oppressive interiors of many of Cruikshank's plates affect in a general way the film's atmospheric rendering of such places as Fagin's den and the Three Cripples.

Cruikshank's strongest influence, however, is on the "look" of particular characters, most notably Fagin, Bill Sikes, Noah Claypole, the Artful Dodger, and Oliver himself. If it is true that, as J. Hillis Miller has noted, "for many readers Fagin, Sikes, Nancy, Oliver, Mr. Brownlow, and Rose Maylie live even more in Cruikshank's etchings than in Dickens's words,"[17] then we must suppose that Cruikshank has in some ways provided a greater inspiration for the visual depiction of the film's characters than does Dickens himself. The film, however, ignores Cruikshank almost entirely in its depiction of Nancy and Mr. Brownlow, and considerably softens the heightened caricature Cruikshank employs to depict a host of other characters. Lean and his collaborators must have shared Henry James's response to Cruikshank's illustrations: James found that the scenes and figures of goodness seemed "more subtly sinister, or more suggestively queer, than the frank badness and horrors."[18] The film's Nancy, therefore, is far prettier (not to mention slimmer), and the film's Brownlow far more benevolent in appearance, than Cruikshank, who was unable or unwilling to draw uneccentric characters, allowed.

In terms of the overall mise-en-scène—of set design, composition, lighting, framing, and so forth—*Oliver Twist* draws on sources that complement and modify the Cruikshank contribution. John Bryan, the production designer who had also worked on *Great Expectations*, exhibits a style imbued with elements of German Expressionist films. Influenced by the Russian-born designer Andrei Andrejew, who, before coming to England in the 1940s, worked in Germany on Robert Wiene's *Raskolnikoff* (1923)—a classic Expressionist film—as well as G. W. Pabst's *Pandora's Box* (1928) and *The Threepenny Opera* (1931), both with settings in Victorian London, Bryan's designs for *Oliver Twist* feature the oblique vistas, exaggerated perspectives, shadowy streets, and oddly tilted buildings characteristic of Expressionist film style. The result is a highly subjective view of London that, in another medium and by different means, reflects Dickens's own subjectivity. Bryan was also inspired, as Andrejew had been before him (notably, in his designs for *The Threepenny Opera*), by the woodcuts of London made by Gustave Doré in 1868–69. Doré's plates captured Victorian London's energy and activity as well as, in his views of the East End, its poverty, darkness, and claustrophobia. Bryan's design of the closely packed roofs of London surrounding Fagin's hide-out—chimney tops everywhere; a curved footbridge in the foreground, the dome of St. Paul's in the background—is a virtual duplication of one of Doré's woodcuts. Some of Doré's other scenes ("Bluegate Fields," "Dudley Street, Seven Dials") provide a more diffuse but nevertheless determining influence on the film's design.

The Expressionist feel of Bryan's sets is supported and amplified by Guy Green's photography and the whole force of Lean's direction. And here, the differences from Cruikshank are as crucial as the similarities. Cruikshank's compositions, for the most part, are "theatrical" in that they allude to the popular stage of the time (Cruikshank, like Dickens, was an instinctive performer and participated in amateur theatricals). Many of his etchings for *Oliver Twist* are composed along horizontal and vertical planes that evoke the box-picture of a proscenium stage: the viewpoint is that of an ideally placed member of a theater audience. His compositions have very little depth, and the background tends to be parallel to the surface of the image. The human figures are frequently "lined up" horizontally (the result can be insipid, as in the drawing of Oliver and Rose Maylie, which Dickens so disliked that he canceled it). There are, of course, exceptions to this pattern. Diagonal lines and a sense of depth play a part in such scenes as "Oliver escapes being bound to a Sweep," "The Evidence Destroyed," "The Meeting," and "The Last Chance," but the tendency, generally, is toward a theatrical space. Lean composes in a very different manner, turning Cruikshank's horizontals and verticals into diagonals, allowing his images to recede into darkness, evoking a threatening and unstable world.

The entire film thus becomes, in a sense, a projection of Oliver's sensibility. Of course, not every scene in the film is tied to Oliver's viewpoint; there are, in fact, many scenes in which Oliver is not present. One must distinguish, as David Bordwell does,[19] between "Impressionist" and "Expressionist" subjectivity: in the former, cutting and camerawork can be read as representing Oliver's perception; in the latter, features of the mise-en-scène can be read as suggesting Oliver's psychological experience of his world. Only at certain specific moments does the film stress Oliver's impressionist point of view. We share his sense of vertigo as he climbs a seemingly endless flight of steps to Fagin's lair, Lean's camera tracking forward ahead of Oliver and tracking back with Oliver in alternating shots as he ascends. A similar technique lends a highly subjective feel to the chase sequence following the attempted robbery of Mr. Brownlow. "Subjectivity" in this sequence is signaled in conventional and obvious ways: Oliver getting socked followed by a brief blackout; Oliver fainting before the magistrate signified by a sharp upward tilt of the camera. In truth, the signifiers for "Impressionist" subjectivity in film are few. But these moments serve their purpose, which is to convince us of the film's pervasive Expressionist subjectivity. And this, in turn, reinforces Lean's emphasis on Oliver as a victim of a threatening and fearful world.

The film's subjectively rendered atmosphere re-creates in a masterly fashion the grim factory world of mid-nineteenth-century Victorian England. The workhouse sequences, in particular, capture a frightened boy's view of the world: overbearing ceilings, entrapping corners, long shadows, oppressive diagonals, backgrounds shrouded in darkness. The sense of claustrophobia so central to the novel ("No novel could be more completely dominated by an imaginative complex of claustrophobia"[20]) receives convincing graphic emphasis from Lean's camera angles, compositions, and lighting. Expressionist shadows punctuate the mise-en-scène: one of the film's most chilling moments occurs during the death watch for Old Sally as her shadow looms against a brick wall. And threatening shadows close in on Nancy as she runs through the dark, wet streets to her fateful meeting with Mr. Brownlow. In the world of Fagin and his accomplices, even the daytime is dark. Bright light takes on symbolic force, so seldom is it evident. When Oliver wakes up at Mr. Brownlow's, all is bright, cheerful, and open; whites are dominant over blacks and grays; horizontals and verticals replace diagonals. Most memorably, perhaps, Lean, in a montage sequence showing the return to normality after a night of terror, follows Dickens in evoking the accusing light that breaks in on Bill Sikes the morning after he has murdered Nancy.

The "look" of *Oliver Twist*, then, is not simply a matter of Cruikshank's illustrations or even of Dickens's text. The film's visual style draws on a rich pictorial tradition that includes Cruikshank but also alludes to Gustave Doré, Hogarth, Piranesi, and the "London" of such German films as *Pandora's Box* and *The Threepenny Opera*. If Lean had only copied Cruikshank or simply (!) illustrated Dickens, he would still have accomplished more than one might suppose. Instead, just as the script's structure both absorbs and reinterprets Dickens's text, wedding it to a tradition of stage and screen melodrama (a tradition from which Dickens himself borrows and which he perpetuates), to an ideological (Soviet) and poetic (Griffith) style of cinematic montage, so too the visual style recapitulates a way of looking at Victorian London that has, in a sense, been absorbed into our cultural memories.

The effect of Lean's various narrative and visual strategies become clearer if we look in some detail at one self-contained sequence of *Oliver Twist*. First, however, it is useful to consider more closely the Eisenstein essay referred to earlier, "Dickens, Griffith, and the Film Today," which analyzes the influence of Dickens's narrative technique and subject matter on D. W. Griffith and on the development of film narrative in general.

"Dickens's nearness to the characteristics of cinema in method, style, and especially in viewpoint and exposition," Eisenstein writes, "is indeed amazing." He points, in particular, to Dickens's "extraordinary plasticity": "The observation in the novel is extraordinary—as is their optical quality. The characters of Dickens are rounded with means as plastic and slightly exaggerated as are the screen heroes of today." Especially, he finds Dickens a master of montage exposition, and in particular the "*montage progression of parallel scenes, intercut into each other*" (emphasis in the original).[21] Eisenstein chooses, among other examples, the episode in *Oliver Twist* where Mr. Brownlow and Mr. Grimwig sit and wait while, in alternating blocks of narrative, Oliver is captured and taken back to Fagin's gang. (Lean, as might be expected, follows Dickens quite closely here; it would have been pointless to do otherwise.) Such broad narrative effects, however, are not limited to Dickens. Perhaps more typical of Dickens, as Eisenstein notes, is "montage," a style that undeniably influenced Lean's treatment of several key episodes. Dickens's montage style, as described by Eisenstein, is evident in the following well-known passage from *Oliver Twist*:

> A council was held; lots were cast who should walk up to the master after supper that evening and ask for more; and it fell to Oliver Twist.
>
> The evening arrived; the boys took their places. The master, in his cook's uniform, stationed himself at the copper; his pauper assistants ranged themselves behind him; the gruel was served out, and a long grace was said over the short commons. The gruel disappeared; the boys whispered each other, and winked at Oliver, while his next neighbours nudged him. Child as he was, he was desperate with hunger, and reckless with misery. He rose from the table, and advancing to the master, basin and spoon in hand, said, somewhat alarmed at his own temerity:
>
> "Please, sir, I want some more."
>
> The master was a fat, healthy man, but he turned very pale. He gazed in stupefied astonishment on the small rebel for some seconds, and then clung for support to the copper. The assistants were paralysed with wonder, the boys with fear.
>
> "What!" said the master at length, in a faint voice.
>
> "Please, sir," replied Oliver, "I want some more."[22]

We should note, especially, Dickens's telegraphic method, achieved through a series of short independent clauses, many of them connected with semicolons. Nearly every clause could be translated into a "shot" with the marks of punctuation becoming cuts, fades, and dissolves. Without slavishly following Dickens's lead, Lean nevertheless takes the hint the text provides and creates from it one of the film's most remarkable sequences, a sequence that expresses and summarizes, almost wordlessly, Oliver's experience in the workhouse. Table 1, which presents a shot-by-shot breakdown of the sequence, suggests something of the richness of Lean's technique.

Table 1—Oliver Asks for More

Shot/Length in Feet	*Description*	*Camera Movement (Movement/Fixed)*
1. (22)	An extreme high angle shot, composed diagonally, of the workhouse courtyard; a group of boys at the top of the frame are filing out of the door into the snow; the curved, spiked supports of the workhouse fence dominate the bottom third of the frame. Music (mimics march of boys). Cut to	F
2. (8)	Medium shot. Oliver center frame, working in a sweat shop with other boys. Music. Dissolve to	F
3. (22)	Close-up of a large kettle and an arm ladling out gruel to boys. Music ends. Dissolve to	F
4. (17)	Long, high shot of the dining area, boys and girls seated at long tables. Dialogue: a voice intones, "For this abounding provision, O Lord, we thank thee."	F
5. (6)	Long, overhead shot of the boardroom, the board members seated around a well-provisioned dinner table. Cut to	F
6. (4)	Close-up of part of the window looking into boardroom, each visible pane occupied by the face of a hungry boy, among them Oliver. Cut to	F
7. (5)	Close shot of a variety of food on boardroom table. Cut to	F
8. (5)	Close shot, at a different angle from shot 6, of more hungry boys at other panes of the same window. Cut to	F
9. (5)	Medium close shot of members of the board eating with gusto, piles of food visible in foreground. Sound: of eating, man on right crunches loudly on a celery stick. Cut to	F
10. (6)	Close shot. Another variation of shot 6. Cut to	F

Table 1—Oliver Asks for More (continued)

Shot/Length in Feet	*Description*	*Camera Movement (Movement/Fixed)*
11. (5)	Close shot, over the shoulder of a board member carrying a large piece of fowl to his mouth and taking a healthy bite. Cut to	F
12. (7)	Full shot of the entire window seen only in part in shots 6, 8, and 10; the boys leave the window. Dissolve to	F
13. (14)	Close-up of a large book (Bible?) with straws between the pages; one boy holds it out as other boys choose straws. Cut to	F
14. (33)	High angle medium shot of boys standing around the boy with the book. A boy draws, and then Oliver, who draws the shortest straw. The other boys exclaim and run off, leaving Oliver, who pauses for a moment and then walks off screen left. Dissolve to	F
15. (28)	Medium shot of the dining room. The camera tracks along the tables left to right and we see the boys and girls at their meal at different tables. The camera continues until it stops at Oliver. Cut to	M
16. (3)	Close shot of 5 boys—two of them highlighted—across the table from Oliver; they regard him expectantly. Cut to	F
17. (13)	Close shot of Oliver finishing his gruel, a boy on either side of him watching his every move.	F
18. (4)	Medium shot of a group of girls looking at Oliver. Cut to	F
19. (7)	Close shot of Oliver, who is not finished with his gruel; he turns his head toward screen left.	F
20. (3)	Medium shot revealing the torso of the Workhouse master with a switch in his hand. Cut to	F

Table 1—Oliver Asks for More (continued)

Shot/Length in Feet	*Description*	*Camera Movement (Movement/Fixed)*
21. (19)	Medium shot of Oliver looking off left, the boys around him looking at him; he rises from his seat and picks up his bowl. Cut to	F
22. (33)	An extreme long shot of Oliver standing next to his table in the depth of the shot; a line of boys are visible along the table right; the bottom half of the master is in the left foreground; Oliver walks toward the camera, which tilts up to include the top half of the master's body. Cut to	M
23. (2)	Close-up of four expectant boys' faces. Cut to	F
24. (7)	Close shot from above of Oliver looking up, bowl in hand. Dialogue: Oliver: "Please, Sir, I want some more." Cut to	F
25. (2)	Full close shot of the master, his face slightly off center screen left. Dialogue: Master: "What?" Cut to	F
26. (1)	Close shot of the matron, her face slightly off center screen right. Dialogue: Matron: "What?" Cut to	F
27. (1)	Tight close shot of Beadle, his face slightly off center screen right. Dialogue: Beadle: "What?" Cut to	F
28. (3)	Medium shot of the board sitting around large table. Dialogue: Head of the Board: "Ask for more?" Dissolve to	F
29. (13)	Close shot of a bill affixed to wall which reads: "£5 and a Boy offered to any tradesman." Music resumes.	F

The montage sequence described in table 1 is, of course, much more elaborate than the passage from Dickens quoted above, even though it consists of a mere three and a half minutes of screen time divided into some thirty shots of varying lengths. At several points Lean alludes with great fidelity to the written text; at the same time, the sequence as a whole cannot simply be equated to that portion of the text from which the quoted paragraphs have been extracted. Lean's montage includes other narrative material from the same chapter; atmospheric detail suggested in the same chapter as well as the preceding and the subsequent chapters; narrative details not present in Dickens's novel (the boys at the window; the board members feasting); transformations or interpretations of narrative materials present in the novel ("lots were cast," Dickens writes; in the film, the boys draw straws); direct discourse rendered in the novel as indirect discourse (the saying of grace in place of Dickens's "a long grace was said over a short commons"); characters not explicitly present in the novel (e.g., the girls in the dining hall); and so forth.

And yet, when all reservations and qualifications have been made, we can assert that the texture of Lean's sequence is remarkably true to the spirit of Dickens. In its structure, in its imagery, in its visual style, in its rhythm, in its arrangement of shots, this montage sequence not only provides a satisfying equivalent to one of the most famous moments in the work of Charles Dickens, but it also recapitulates the tone and flavor of the novel and at the same time encapsulates the visual and narrative strategies of the film as a whole. The alternating montage of hungry boys and well-fed officials, if not in Dickens, is precisely Dickensian in its technique. The (discontinuous) sequence of three shots of boys looking through a window at a feast in which they cannot partake—first one group, then another, then both groups together—unites the boys in a common misery. The low-angle shot of Oliver at the rear of a dark, obliquely composed dining hall constructed of iron and brick, subsumes the entire first quarter of the novel; the large, comically exaggerated, similarly composed close-ups of the master, the matron, and Mr. Bumble, edited in rapid succession as each cries, "What?" establishes these figures as symbols of repression and objects of laughter in a manner parallel to Dickens's best style of grotesque caricature.

We may further note that Lean's sequence alludes to without precisely imitating Cruikshank's illustration of "Oliver asking for More." Cruikshank, as is usual in his most effective plates, captures not only the moment but the attendant circumstances as well: we could, in a sense, reconstruct Dickens's narrative from the illustration. The style and composition, however, are very unlike Lean's handling. The view, once again, is theatrical: the edges of the drawing entirely contain the action. A horrified female pauper stands extreme left, behind the large kettle; next to her, the master of the workhouse faces down and toward the right; Oliver, presenting the opposite profile, looks up at the master; in the shallow background, the boys are in various stages of emptying their bowls, licking their spoons and fingers and/or looking at Oliver with amazement, apprehension, and fear. This, of course, is just the kind of stage picture Lean avoids. Whereas Cruikshank's is an "objective," two-dimensional, eye-level viewpoint of the ideally placed but detached observer, Lean's point of view is subjective, oddly angled, composed in depth and, of course, fragmented through editing. And yet Cruikshank undeniably influenced Lean's presentation of the boys' faces and manner, the appearance and stance of Oliver, the expression on the master's face, the set and the lighting, and, in general, the dynamics of the entire sequence.

Oliver Twist, then, is a creative interpretation of a literary text *and* a visual tradition, both of which influence without dominating almost every aspect of the film. These influences have their effect even on the performances of Lean's uniformally fine cast. The acting style is presentational; subtlety gives way to the broad and calculated effects required by the somewhat Grand Guignol world of Dickens's tale. Robert Newton, who could, on occasion, show restraint (as he does, memorably, in *This Happy Breed*), lets out all of the stops for Bill Sikes, squinting one eye and shaking with anger in his best melodramatic manner. And the effect, somehow, is just right: Bill Sikes is both malevolent and comic (but not funny—one does not laugh at Sikes), a frightening, eccentric figure. (By contrast, Oliver Reed, in Carol Reed's *Oliver* [1968], gives a naturalistic performance that captures the malevolence but loses much of the eccentricity.) As Nancy, Kay Walsh is quite moving, balancing vulgarity, sensuality, and a good heart while avoiding the sentimental decorations with which Dickens finally smothers her. Oliver is ideally portrayed by John Howard Davies, who would be so effective in *The Rocking-Horse Winner* (1949). His thin body, long, narrow face, and wistful, wide-eyed expression, which remains virtually unchanging throughout, renders perfectly the somewhat aristocratic, vulnerable, mostly passive role Oliver plays in his own story. Other characters—Bumble, Sowerberry, Brownlow, the Artful Dodger, all the way down to the smallest role—are invested with iconographic substance inspired by Dickens's shorthand methods of characterization.

And then we come to Alec Guinness's Fagin. "Fagin in Berlin Provokes a Riot," proclaimed *Life* magazine (7 March 1949, pp. 38–39): "On two successive nights the Jews and police fought with clubs, rocks and fire-hoses around the Kurbel Theater in Berlin's British sector. . . . Before riots ended 35 Jews had been injured and three arrested. Seven policemen were hurt." Caption: "Scenes from a picture Americans cannot see." Caption: "Fagin is presented in 'Oliver Twist' exactly as he was described by Charles Dickens." The *New York Times* (10 September 1948, p. 19): "The New York Board of Rabbis ask Eric Johnston, president of the Motion Picture Producers Association, to keep *Oliver Twist* out of the U.S., describing the film—sight unseen—as a 'vehicle of blatant anti-Semitism.'" *Time* (4 October 1948, p. 96): "Last week [J. Arthur] Rank announced that the U.S. release [of *Oliver Twist*] would be 'indefinitely postponed.'"

Fagin and the boys welcome Oliver in Oliver Twist.

Complex issues are evoked by the above news items, issues that cannot be entered into in any great detail here. Several ironies might be noted, however: *Oliver Twist*, one of those rare British films with a potential to thrive in the American market, is banned (for a time) from the United States altogether; Fagin, who is referred to as a Jew some 300 times in the novel, is never so identified in the film (but, of course, everyone "knows" Fagin is a Jew—from reading the novel if from nothing else); *Life* is not precisely correct in claiming that "Fagin is presented in 'Oliver Twist' exactly as he was described by Charles Dickens." The following, ambiguous sentence from the same article, may be more accurate: "Director David Lean pleaded guilty only to fidelity to Dickens, pointing out that he had molded his characters on the Cruikshank illustrations."

"Fidelity to Dickens . . . the Cruikshank illustrations"; as we have already suggested, these are not necessarily equivalent. Alec Guinness's makeup is true to Cruikshank; Dickens's description of Fagin is much less specific: "a very old shrivelled Jew, whose villainous-looking and repulsive face was obscured by a quantity of matted red hair."[23] The red hair was one of the accouterments of stage Jews in Dickens's time; otherwise, the description is not stereotypically "Jewish." Later, it is true, Dickens indirectly alludes to the size of Fagin's nose. But Cruikshank, himself influenced by a British tradition of portraying Ashkenazic Jews (see Hogarth's Jewish peddler in plate 2 of his Election Series), clearly inspired the makeup that nearly obliterates Guinness's face: huge nose, thick lips, hooded eyes, a scraggly beard. To this, Guinness added a low, gravelly voice, a lisp, and a vaguely Eastern European intonation and accent. His performance, as distinct from his appearance, is true to Dickens's characterization, though the film (another irony) tends to soften Fagin, who is more sinister and malevolent in the novel. Guinness adds a touch of sympathy and humor all his own; in his hands, the "pickpocket lesson" takes on the character of a droll music-hall turn. Certainly, Guinness provides a caricature of a Jew, though his Jew is not as "evil" as in the novel and not as "evil" (which is also true of Dickens's Fagin) as Bill Sikes or Monks, who are not Jews.

Is Lean's film anti-Semetic? This, it seems to me, cannot be demonstrated. Lean's defense is reasonable: the film can only be objectionable to the extent that the novel is. On the other hand, Lean and company were, at the least, not as sensitive to the issue as they might have been, and the British authorities who allowed the film to be shown in postwar, occupied Berlin were certainly lacking in judgment. It is nevertheless inexcusable that the film was banned in the United States until 1951, when an edited version, twelve minutes shorter than the original, was released. Gone was the scene where Fagin goes through his treasure box and is seen by Oliver; the first scene with Monks was shortened (making this part of the plot nearly incomprehensible); various brief shots, mostly close-ups of Fagin, were trimmed throughout. It is this censored version that is publicly exhibited in the United States to this day (as at a New York showing at the Thalia Theater in December 1981). The censors, for all practical purposes, have won.

Between the release of *Great Expectations* and *Oliver Twist,* Lean found time to reflect. Writing in *Penguin Film Review,* he looks back with pride on the achievements of British films in the postwar period and expects more of the same. He has high praise for the methods of his boss, J. Arthur Rank.

> We of Independent Producers can make any subject we wish, with as much money as we think that subject should have spent on it. We can cast whatever actors we choose, and we have no interference at all in the way the film is made. No one sees the films until they are finished, and no cuts are made without the consent of the Director or Producer, and what's more, not one of us is bound by any form of contract. We are there because we want to be there . . . such are the conditions which have at last given our films a style and nationality of their own.[24]

This seemingly ideal condition, however, would not last much longer. Shortly after the release of *Oliver Twist,* Rank announced that his organization's bank loans and overdrafts stood at £13,589,858. It was crisis time once again.

5

Lean and Ann Todd

NINETEEN FORTY-EIGHT to 1952 were transitional years for Lean both personally and professionally. He successively directed three films featuring Ann Todd, a major British star following the popular success of Compton Bennett's *The Seventh Veil* in 1945. Between the first and second film of this loose trilogy, Lean married his leading lady; between the second and third, he moved from the Rank Organization to Alexander Korda's London Films. *The Passionate Friends* (1949) and *Madeleine* (1950), probably the least-known and least-appreciated of Lean's films, were released in an atmosphere of ever-worsening crisis for British films. "In February of 1949 only seven of the twenty-six British film studios were in operation and only eleven films were actually being made. . . . In March 1949 the forty-five per cent quota was reduced to thirty per cent, a move to placate the Americans."[1] Both comparatively offbeat, Lean's latest films did not please either the critics or the public. (Another Cineguild film, Marc Allegret's *Blanche Fury,* also failed at the box office.) By the time *Madeleine* was released, Cineguild had broken up and one of the more glorious chapters in the history of the British cinema had come to an end.

Lean stayed with Rank another six months, planning a film on Mary, Queen of Scots, as a vehicle for Ann Todd. When difficulties arose over budget, Lean left the Rank fold to join Alexander Korda's London Films. His move was typical. Between 1946 and 1955 "almost a dozen of Britain's best film-makers were to migrate from the Rank Organisation to Korda's British Lion–London Films outfit."[2] Among them were Carol Reed, Powell and Pressburger, Launder and Gilliat, and Laurence Olivier. Korda, who had been temporarily in eclipse, now replaced Rank as Britain's top producer/financier. In moving over to Korda, Lean very likely lost some of his independence (though he remained his own producer); he certainly worked under tightened budgetary restrictions. Nevertheless, his first film for Korda, *The Sound Barrier,* to some extent recouped his tarnished reputation.

Ann Todd and Norman Wooland in Madeleine.

The Passionate Friends, *Madeleine*, and *The Sound Barrier* all exploit, to varying degrees, the neurotic intensity and cool, almost regal demeanor that constitutes Ann Todd's distinctive acting personality. In both *The Passionate Friends* and *Madeleine*, she plays characters who struggle mightily for independence even as their passionate natures threaten to betray them. Romance for them, as for many of Lean's heroines, becomes a form of self-entrapment. In both roles, Todd is very much at the center of our interest and concern. In *The Sound Barrier*, however, Lean, perhaps in response to box-office realities, relegates his wife to a subsidiary position, enclosing her safely within the film's diegetic outlines rather than allowing her, as in the two previous films, to spill out of it. Todd's performance consequently suffers: reduced to a conventional persona, she can make little use of the intelligence and cool sensuality that complicate and enrich her screen presence. In thus demoting her, Lean temporarily abandons complex romantic themes for a primarily masculine world of adventure and technology.

The Passionate Friends (1948)

Eric Ambler's screenplay for *The Passionate Friends* bears only the slightest and most oblique relationship to its source. In his 1913 novel of the same title, H. G. Wells had placed a love story against a backdrop of large social and historical events. The Boer War, the labor issue, the peace movement, and, most especially, the Woman Question, contribute matter for what is in reality a novel of ideas disguised as romance. Virtually unread today, the novel is both intriguing and slight. While we may admire Wells's progressive social and political views, we are disappointed by his failure to integrate the private and public themes or to make his characters seem much more than symbols. Lean's film ignores the broad social issues and in fact retains little of the novel apart from the central romantic situation, a triangular relationship among Steven, Mary, and her husband, Justin (Howard in the film). Of Wells's larger purposes, only one—but it is a crucial one—remains: the insistence on a woman's need to remain independent even from a man she deeply loves. Surprisingly, this theme makes *The Passionate Friends*, which Ambler placed in the present, more mature and innovative than most films released in the late 1940s. What strikes us as progressive in a 1913 novel still appears so (appears even more so?) in a 1948 film; in fact, it still seems progressive today.

Lean situates Mary Justin (Ann Todd) at the center of the film and makes her consciousness his unifying theme. While in the novel Stephen is the narrator, Mary narrates most of the film's events, interweaving present and past associations, incorporating flashbacks within flashbacks, combining imagination and reality. This unusually complex narrative mode

Claude Rains and Ann Todd in The Passionate Friends.

sets up reverberations among present and past events that break down accepted categories like cause and effect, before and after, now and then. As he will do, somewhat differently, in *Lawrence of Arabia,* Lean opens *The Passionate Friends* with a flashback narrative that is never really "closed." Mary's story has no specific auditor, no clearly defined occasion. The film never takes us to that point where Mary's narrative began. In effect, we have immediate, if sporadic, access to Mary's thoughts. Her internal monologue becomes a subtext that both enriches and undermines the narrative proper.

Unraveled and retold chronologically, *The Passionate Friends* would look something like this. Steve Stratton (Trevor Howard), a young biologist, loves and is loved by Mary Christian (as she is called in the novel: no maiden name is given in the film). He asks her to be his wife, but Mary, unwilling to give up her independence, resists his overtures and instead marries Howard Justin (Claude Rains), a successful banker who neither expects nor demands that Mary "belong" to him. Some years later, Steven and Mary meet by chance and resume their romance. Initially, Mary seems as unwilling as ever to be possessed, to give herself over entirely to love, but as the affair intensifies, she weakens: "I shall belong to you," she tells Steven. At this point, Howard discovers the affair and confronts Mary and Steven with his knowledge. Steven wants Mary to leave her husband, but she chooses, for reasons never made explicit, to stay with Howard and agrees never to see her lover again. Nine years go by. Mary, awaiting her husband's arrival at a Swiss resort where they are vacationing, learns that Steven occupies the adjoining room. They spend an "innocent" day together and once again separate, Mary regretfully aware that Steven has found happiness elsewhere. Howard finds out about the meeting and, putting the worse construction on it, initiates divorce proceedings. In order to avoid scandal for herself and for Steven, and in despair over the emptiness of her life, Mary contemplates suicide. Rescued at the last moment by Howard, Mary for the first time realizes the depth of his love for her and—presumably—reconciles herself to her marriage and her life.

The film-text arranges these events into a somewhat different pattern. The distinct movements and time-shifts could be enumerated as follows. (1) Mary arrives in Switzerland and her voice-over narration begins; the time is indefinite but close, as we subsequently discover, to the film's present. Steven arrives at the same hotel that same evening, but the two of them do not yet meet. (2) Mary's first flashback takes us back to New Year's Eve, 1938–39. Steven and Mary, who is married, meet by chance at a ball; they have not seen each other for some time. (Logically, this flashback should have been triggered off by Mary's encounter with Steven in Switzerland, although that encounter has not yet—in terms of what we have seen—taken place.) Leaving the ball with her husband, Mary, seated in the back of her chauffeured automobile, slips into reverie, initiating another flashback within the first flashback. (3) Mary and Steven sit at the edge of a lake and talk intimately; the time is indefinite, but clearly in the early stages of their romance. (4) We come back to Mary, brought out of her reverie by the car's jolting movement. (5) Mary slips back into her memories, and a new flashback begins. The time is again uncertain, but Steven and Mary still act like ardent young lovers. (6) A sound cut—the car door opening—takes us back to Mary arriving home after the New Year's Eve party. (7) Later that same night, lying in bed, Mary again loses herself in memory. The time of this flashback is uncertain. Mary and Steven argue; she tells him that she does not want to be possessed by anyone. "Then," he responds, "your life will be a failure." (8) Back to Mary's bed, as Steven's words reverberate in her consciousness.

Now, a new episode (9) begins, unannounced by Mary's narration. The time is presumably soon after the New Year's Eve party. Steven calls Mary and they begin an affair, which her husband discovers. Mary agrees never to see Steven again. (10) We are back in Switzerland, near the point where Mary's first flashback began. Mary and Steven meet and spend the day together (during which Mary at several moments imagines, through subjective inserts, that the love affair has been renewed); they part. Howard arrives. (11) Back in England, Howard sues for divorce. From this point on, the film moves chronologically to its conclusion. Mary's voice-over, however, resumes briefly but does not "close" the film, which ends immediately after Howard forestalls Mary's suicide attempt.

In constructing his film so as to emphasize Mary's consciousness, Lean creates a deeply enigmatic text, one told almost entirely from the viewpoint of a character who, although at the center of her own narrative, remains essentially mysterious. Actually, matters are more complicated than that. The objective and the subjective coexist in the film, as they must in any film purporting to be a first-person narrative. (A seeming exception, Robert Montgomery's *Lady in the Lake* [1946], actually proves the rule: the consistent use of a "subjective" camera results in the virtual elimination of all true subjectivity.) In *The Passionate Friends* (entitled *One Woman's Story* in the United States), we frequently see things Mary could not have seen, and we sometimes experience as objective reality what Mary may be merely imagining. Throughout the film, we are thus aware of two narrations, Mary's and the camera's. These are seldom, if ever, truly congruent. The film's first few moments present a mild tension between what Mary says and what she sees. Mary stands on the porch of her hotel room during a portion of her voice-over narration. As she speaks the words, "I suppose I was aware that there was an adjoining room," she walks back into her own room. The camera starts to follow her, but almost immediately tracks toward the left and enters the adjoining room—later to be occupied by Steven—and comes to rest framed on the bed. In a sense, the camera—though technically violating her literal point of view—completes Mary's thought process, "acts out" what she is thinking, enacts her desire, anticipates the direction of her narrative. The film, in effect, deliberately confuses conscious and unconscious realms. Lean seems to abdicate his responsibility for the narrative while asserting his control over it.

In consequence, the tension between objective and subjective, between the romantic and the everyday, becomes in itself a theme—as it is, to some degree, in all of Lean's love stories. Mary's first flashback-within-a-flashback begins with a luminous, shimmering dreamlike image of Steven and Mary. We assume, reasonably, that the shimmer is a dissolve, a sign for "flashback." Actually, we are looking at images of Steven and Mary reflected on a lake's surface. When Steven throws a stone into the water, the lovers disappear beneath a ripple of circles. The fragility, the insubstantiality, of romantic love is signified at the same time that an idyllic aura surrounds it. Mary's vision is both real and unreal, substantial and imaginary. This brief insert serves multiple functions. Prefiguring the whole subsequent development of the narration, it also confuses diegetic and nondiegetic realms, beginning and ending with a "dissolve" that is part of the diegesis rather than, as with most cinematic dissolves, apart from it. An image (a series of images) can be simultaneously subjective and objective, part of the discourse and a comment on the discourse. The flashback is Mary's, but it is as well the film's (Lean's). Furthermore, visual links connect the images in this insert with parts of other images in the film that are not necessarily included in Mary's consciousness. The branches and leaves that shadow the lovers' faces, for example, prefigure the branches glimmering in the sunlight at the beginning of Mary's next reverie, and, with less pointed association, the branches that throw their shadows on Mary as she lies in bed on New Year's Eve as well as the shadows on the hotel beds in the film's opening sequence. By such devices, Lean suggests that in his heroine's consciousness past, present, and imaginary are not separate realms but rather various fragments of truth coexisting in each moment of time.

Lean's stylistic flourishes deepen the enigma of Mary Justin's character, transforming the elements of a conventional romantic melodrama, complete with guilty adulterers and a jealous husband, into the study of a highly unusual heroine. With Mary's character, the film directly touches on the novel. Of H. G. Wells's dialogue, perhaps no more than two lines find their way into the film, and both are Mary's: "I want to belong to myself" and "Why can't there be love without this clutching, this gripping?" Taken together, these become the key to Mary's character and actions, explaining how she can reject her lover and cling instead to a loveless marriage. In the film, somewhat more than in the novel, Mary also wants a comfortable life, but this is not seen to be paramount. Mary's desire for independence seems at times perverse and self-defeating; the film suggests strongly that it is both. Mary wants life on her own terms, and her defeat follows inevitably. Wells was himself unable to save her: in the novel, she commits suicide. The film rescues her, but only by reestablishing her marriage. This is not entirely a defeat for Mary, however. Her husband—who, unlike the novel's husband, turns out to be a decent man—discovers that he truly loves her, and the marriage, from what we have seen of it, has at least the potential for allowing Mary the freedom she needs. Nevertheless, the film ends ambiguously. What does Mary feel in that final close-up? We cannot really know. Her narration, which might answer the question, has abruptly ended. The film could not contain her viewpoint and so had to abort her narration. *The Passionate Friends* thus carries us beyond Mary's consciousness, but it posits nothing in its place.

Neither a commercial nor a critical success, *The Passionate Friends* may have failed for the very reason that makes it interesting today: the enigma that lies at the heart of Mary's character. Lean's heroine was perhaps too cool, too confused, too "perverse" to be at the center of a 1940s love story.

Clearly intrigued by Mary's (and Todd's) mystery, Lean cannot penetrate it anymore than we. The film's primary interest thus becomes the tension between its fairly conventional story and its unconventional narration. If, by the end, the film's unraveling betrays Mary, nullifying her yearning for independence, recouping her within the bounds of a conventional marriage, positioning her among the mores and social requirements of the later 1940s, Lean's structuring in effect denies the full force of that movement and holds in a kind of temporal solution Mary's rebelliousness and individuality, qualities that the mere development of plot cannot finally obliterate.

Madeleine (1950)

One of the most intriguing of Lean's lesser-known films, *Madeleine* reconstructs the substance of a celebrated Victorian murder trial. In 1857, a young Scotswoman, Madeleine Smith, was accused of poisoning her lover and tried by a Glasgow court. Unable to determine her guilt or innocence, the jury returned the uniquely Scottish verdict, "not proven." Madeleine was set free, but a judicial shadow hung over her for the remainder of her life. In adapting this material for the screen, Lean and his writers made a decision that, as it turned out, may have been fatal to the film's commercial chances. Rather than "solve" the crime themselves by inventing a plausible set of circumstances one way or the other, they chose to retain the ambiguities and confusions that had made it impossible for the original jury to reach a decisive verdict. As in *The Passionate Friends*, Lean here makes ambiguity itself the theme. Consequently, *Madeleine* for the most part eschews the dynamics of a conventional courtroom melodrama and becomes, at least during its first two-thirds, a study of female sexuality within a Victorian context. Unfortunately, insofar as it does eventually become a courtroom drama, the film frustrates an audience's normal desire and expectation to be let in on the secret that history has failed to reveal.

Lean, in short, effected a trade-off, sacrificing the satisfaction of solving the crime for the opportunity to study a potentially fascinating woman. *Madeleine* is thus both an ambiguous film and a film about ambiguity. Lean explores and develops a series of contrasts and contradictions, examining the Victorian milieu through a modern sensibility, stressing the paradox inherent in the situation of a proper, intelligent woman giving herself up to a seemingly cheap and sordid affair, hinting at a connection between sexual license and repressed incestuous impulses, and demonstrating the destructive force of romantic passion. In *Madeleine*, as in several of Lean's other films, illicit romance signifies rebellion against stultifying convention; for a woman, in particular, this is often the only form of rebellion possible. Romance, however, turns out to be another trap, another convention as restrictive in its own way as the one his—particularly female—lovers seek to escape. *Madeleine* concerns itself with this major paradox.

Once again, Lean employs an overt narrative framework. The film begins with a lengthy pan of modern-day Glasgow under the credits. At the end of the credits, Lean cuts to a specific house, "the home of Madeleine Smith": "her strange romantic story," a voice-over narrator tells us, "has survived the elegance of the house she lived in." We are explicitly being told a "tale," a well-known story reshaped in cinematic form. The film's opening immediately presents contrasts: a once elegant but now shabby house and a "strange romantic story" from the past related by a present-day narrator. The house, as we quickly discover, plays a symbolic role. When the discourse proper begins, the Smith family (father, mother, and three daughters, of whom Madeleine is the oldest), on a house-hunting expedition, enter it for the first time. While exploring the house, Madeleine seems drawn, almost mystically, to a large basement room. This basement becomes her bedroom (she shares it with the youngest daughter); here, late at night, she meets her lover, Emile. (The narrative structure of these early scenes makes it unclear whether Madeleine knew Emile before her family moved into the new house; we do not, in any case, ever find out how they met or when.) Madeleine's immediate fascination with the dark, isolated basement both suggests her strong need to escape from the Victorian family hearth and symbolically expresses the subterranean emotions of this seemingly proper, well-brought-up Scottish woman. In simple Freudian terms, the basement houses Madeleine's id, the upper rooms her superego. Lean constructs a comparable architectural arrangement for the trial sequences later in the film. Each time she appears in court, Madeleine must make her entrance from the courthouse basement through a trapdoor. She is being tried, in effect, for living in that basement.

In *Madeleine*, the conflict between id and superego finds social expression as a tension between spontaneity and form. The Victorian setting brings out this tension especially well. In several scenes, Lean makes us aware of how the elaborate nineteenth-century bustles and petticoats both distort and lend a mysterious excitement to female sexuality. When, for example, Madeleine, preparing to meet her lover, scurries around in her heavily petticoated gown as she puts out the lights, Lean's gliding camera, which briskly follows her movements, evokes a particularly exquisite eroticism. (How long it must have taken, we marvel, to remove all of those clothes.) Later in the film, after Madeleine's father has discovered his daughter's affair, he can only express his sense of disgust and shame by saying simply, "We are naked."

Mr. Smith's response to his daughter's sexuality suggests the clearly sexual tension in their relationship, a tension due in part to the repressive atmosphere of the Smith household. Mr. Smith (beautifully played by Leslie Banks), an archetypal Victorian paterfamilias, rules his family by the sheer force of a cold, overbearing will. His nightly ritual of bidding his daughters goodnight by kissing each chastely on the forehead, sometimes adding a piece of fatherly advice ("You bolted your food tonight: do not, every mouthful should be chewed"), perfectly encapsulates the distance between feeling and form. Indirectly, Lean hints at a strong, unexpressed bond between father and daughter. One scene in particular brings this out forcefully. Wishing to speak to her about the desirability of her marrying, Smith tells Madeleine to remove his boots as they talk. Complying, Madeleine kneels at his feet, her dress spreading out on the floor beneath her. Lean, maintaining a tight frame on both characters, photographs much of the ensuing conversation from behind Leslie Banks' head, stressing the father's overbearing position and the daughter's soft, pliant vulnerability. The dialogue, too, is charged. "There seems to be something about your character," Smith tells Madeleine, "that prevents you from acting naturally." The implication of these words, an implication the scene in its entirety supports, is that Madeleine's character is disturbingly sexual and her "unnatural" behavior a provocation. Smith's anxiety to marry his daughter off expresses his need to exorcise the effect she has on him. Marriage will allow Madeleine to act naturally by forcing her to become a proper Victorian wife. For her part, Madeleine has internalized her father's hold on her, making him an object of both fear and love. Lean stresses the complexities of the relationship by dissolving from the scene where Madeleine breaks off with Emile to a glamorous ball where she dances with her father. Moments later, she accepts the proposal of the man her father wants her to marry.

The sexual element in Madeleine's character and her revolt against conventional bourgeois forms come together when she performs a Highland dance with her lover Emile. Both in terms of emotional intensity and technical assurance, this is one of the best moments in Lean's films. The sequence begins with Madeleine and Emile standing on a bluff looking down on a small village. Captivated by the music from a dance taking place down below, Madeleine begins to move to the rhythm. By degrees she seduces the reluctant Emile into dancing with her. As she demonstrates the steps for him, he tries to imitate her as best he can, but he lacks the requisite grace and energy. Lean intercuts shots of the village dance, which becomes progressively louder and more uninhibited, and singles out a particularly attractive and sensual pair. Madeleine, too, becomes freer and more provocative in her movements. She suddenly grabs Emile's ever-present walking stick ("You can't dance with that in your hand") and tosses it aside. Emile stops dancing and holds her wrist, but she pulls away, throwing herself on the ground. Emile approaches her as she looks up expectantly at him; he smiles and leans toward her. Lean cuts to the village dance, which has become quite wild. The young couple singled out earlier become more and more excited by the frenzy of the dance, finally running out of the hall together as the music ends. Fade to black.

The sequence is a tour de force, but that should not distract us from its several significances. Lean, by giving us an unambiguous if metaphoric expression of Madeleine's sensuality, insists on the sexual nature of this love affair. The scene's meaning becomes even clearer later in the film when Madeleine, having finally agreed to marry Mr. Minnoch, her dignified and approved suitor, dances a sedate Cumberland reel with him as the rejected Emile watches from the shadows. Furthermore, Madeleine performs her passionate Highland fling virtually alone, for her lover, though he may be necessary to the dance, makes an inadequate partner, being himself a slave to convention who yearns not to transcend dour Victorian society but to join it. Like most of Lean's women, Madeleine is clearly the dominant partner, the possessor of the romantic spirit whose yearnings cannot be satisfied by any actual, flesh-and-blood lover.

This last point helps to explain and justify Emile's seeming unworthiness as object of Madeleine's affection and passion. Indeed, before we have a clear sense of the film's direction, the problem appears to be one of casting. Ivan Desny, who plays Emile, acts out an Englishman's idea of a Frenchman. Somewhat oily, fastidiously overdressed, he does not strike us as either attractive or interesting. The French lover, we are bound to feel, does not seem very different from the unwelcome Scottish suitor (who is, in fact, a handsome and kind man). Soon, however, it becomes clear that Emile is meant to be unworthy of Madeleine's love. His interest in Madeleine, for one thing, turns out to be far more mercenary than we had at first supposed. What initially seemed a casting error was actually a deliberate choice. We are thrown back on trying to fathom the depths of Madeleine's emotions. What does she see in him, we wonder. By virtue of his nationality and social status, he is an exotic and an outsider who provides a conduit for her suppressed desires. Otherwise, he is a poor match. Typically, when Emile discovers Madeleine in his room, the first thing he says is, "What has brought you here?" whereas her first words are, "Put your arms around me."

The difficulty in pinning down Madeleine's character cannot be separated from our response to Ann Todd. As in *The Passionate Friends*, she here plays a woman who on the one hand exhibits a forceful independence of spirit while on the other hand she seems virtually trapped by her dependence on men. Just as Mary Justin, in the earlier film, refused to destroy the delicate balance of her relationship with her (fatherlike) husband for the sake of her lover, so Madeleine cannot bring herself to tell her dominating father that she desires to marry a man he would not approve of. In *Madeleine*, Todd gives a subtle and complex performance, but she frequently seems to be working against the grain of her character. Her tone often suggests a woman who ought to be above—or at least apart from—the melodramatic goings-on it is her lot to act out. Similarly, though she is in many ways a lovely woman, her somewhat pinched face and cool manner, together with the obvious fact that she is rather older than the character she portrays, complicates our response to Madeleine Smith's passion. Has Lean misjudged the nature and extent of his wife's allure? Perhaps. And yet the final effect, it seems to me, is an enrichment of Madeleine's character. For the result of the seeming contradictions between the actress and the role provides a neurotic coloring, an added strangeness to the "strange romantic story" the narrator has promised us.

My discussion thus far might lead a reader to suppose that *Madeleine* is a more interesting film—more subtle, complex, and ambiguous—than it really is. Actually, if I may be allowed a paradox of my own, *Madeleine is* more interesting than it really is. The problem is that *Madeleine,* like *The Passionate Friends,* has within itself two films, neither of which is entirely satisfactory. The first film, the one I have been describing, explores dark corners of human behavior. The other film is an unresolved murder mystery. The two are not truly integrated, and perhaps could not have been given the decision to leave the question of Madeleine's guilt open-ended. Both character and plot remain unresolved. As the murder story takes over, Lean indulges in a variety of mystifications and portents that suggest we are going to discover something that, in fact, we never do. A Hitchcock-like close-up of a cocoa cup, for example, serves no purpose but to mislead and confuse the audience since not only do we not know whether it contains poison but no one in the film even suspects that it might. It is only the film, as it were, that is suspicious. (Similar close-ups of cups and glasses in Alfred Hitchcock's *Notorious* and *Suspicion* are meaningful because someone in the film suspects, rightly in one case and wrongly in the other, that these objects might contain poison and because both we and the potential victim eventually find out the truth). And much the same objection could be made to the last quarter or so of the film, which, in spite of some fine moments, simply deepens the mystification. Surprisingly, the tension actually lets up once Madeleine is put on trial, and the conventional elements of a courtroom drama replace the earlier concerns with psychological complexities, concerns that, in spite of its flaws, make *Madeleine* a frequently rich and mature film.

The Sound Barrier (1952)

The Sound Barrier, Lean's third and final film starring Ann Todd, provides some ammunition to those critics who wish to dismiss Lean as a mere "technician." For one thing, the film is as much about technology as it is about anything else, and it exhibits as well a strong impulse toward documentary. Much of the film cannot, in fact, be distinguished from documentary either in look or in tone: the aerial footage and the frankly explanatory dialogue create a texture reminiscent of educational films. The film's original audience was impressed primarily with its documentary elements, its evocation of reality. And the scenes in the air, filmed by a second unit but carefully edited by Lean and Geoffrey Foot, remain impressive even today, long after space exploration (as well as routine jet travel) has numbed our responses to something as mundane as flying at the speed of sound.

The Sound Barrier succeeds particularly well at capturing (and, for a present-day audience, recapturing) a sense of what speed *feels* like. A shot of a jet coming toward us juxtaposed through editing to a shot of the same plane going away from us precisely evokes the psychological effect of speed. The sound editing works with the images to intensify this effect. As a jet speeds toward the camera, the sound of its engine is slightly delayed, increasing in intensity as the plane disappears. In one particularly striking shot, we see only the results of the plane's force and speed disturbing the surface of a wheatfield; the sound comes in a beat later. (Lean, in a sense, cheats here: we should not be seeing the plane before we hear it, since it has yet to fly faster than sound.) *The Sound Barrier* creates a subjective impression of speed and power that reveals Lean to be an extremely lyrical technician indeed. For him and for us, the de Havilland *Comet* and *Vampire* and the Vickers *Swift* and *Attacker* are not simply machines but objects of beauty and grace.

"While it remains in the air," one critic writes, "*The Sound Barrier* is a superb film."[3] As this comment implies, Lean's film does not succeed in balancing its documentary with its dramatic elements. The problem, however, might be stated the other way around. The film spends too much time in the air and not enough on the ground, substituting a celebration of technology for a meaningful engagement with the human dilemma that that very technology has brought about. It is almost as if the film were enacting a questionable aspect of its own thematic project by preferring the self-indulgence and "purity" of flight to the difficulties of solid earth. Terence Rattigan's script seems to descend too often into glibness and cliché in part because the film's structure gives the dialogue sequences too little weight and energy. Clichés can be redeemed by applying to them the pressure of sincerity, something Lean seems unable or unwilling to do.

In its early sequences, *The Sound Barrier* promises to be a much more interesting film than it turns out to be: during the first twenty minutes, Lean establishes a potentially complex dynamic of personalities, ethical issues, and visual patterns. The precredit sequence reveals, in a few panning shots, wartime shore batteries on the Dover coast. The sound of an airplane catches the attention of a squad of soldiers. And then the plane itself, a Spitfire, appears, swoops up and up, seemingly turns somersaults, and finally plunges into a free fall. A close shot of the pilot; his plane begins to vibrate; a tense moment; he pulls it out; the Spitfire soars once again; first title: *The Sound Barrier.* In quick succession, we are introduced to the major characters and conflicts: Philip Peel (John Justin), the young pilot of the precredit sequence, destined to "break" the sound barrier; Tony Garthwaite (Nigel Patrick), also a pilot, pleasant, charming, superficial; Susan Ridgefield (Ann Todd), Tony's sweetheart and very soon his wife; Susan's father, John Ridgefield (Ralph Richardson), aviation pioneer and aircraft manufacturer; Susan's younger brother, Chris (Denholm Elliott), the weak son of a powerful father. Ridgefield, a stern, overbearing man, is entirely absorbed by his dream of conquering space, of imposing technology on the universe. He shows little affection for either of his children (both of whom admire him but find him difficult to love), but he immediately takes to his new son-in-law, Tony.

The tensions and configurations established early in the film are brilliantly projected in the scene where Ridgefield shows off his "secret," jet propulsion, to Tony as his son and daughter watch. The design of the engine itself and the way Lean photographs it emphasize its phallic power. The camera tracks admiringly along its tubular length as the test begins with an explosive "whoosh." The test is treated by Ridgefield like a ritual, a revelation of mysteries. The effect of all of this is reflected in the attitude and expressions of each character. Ridgefield and Tony, the "masculine" pair, are in the engine room; Susan and Chris watch from behind a screen. Ridgefield, who may, in psychoanalytic terms, be said to *be* the phallus, is, of course, proud: this is his baby. Tony, the new son, the "real" son, is excited, enthusiastic, and fascinated. Susan, too, is excited, but also disturbed and apprehensive. Chris is similarly at once intrigued and intimidated: his earlier resolve to tell his father that he does not want to be a flier evaporates in face of this overwhelming force. The following morning, Chris is killed during his first solo flight. Susan blames her father for his death, while Tony is "adopted" by the father-in-law he admires.

Unfortunately, Lean and Rattigan do not develop the possibilities suggested by this early scene. Having introduced a number of promising themes, they either fail to establish them clearly or close off discussion in an unsatisfactory manner. The tension between male and female roles, for example, strongly foregrounded in both *The Passionate Friends* and *Madeleine*, is here reduced to a banal 1950s conflict between the masculine imperative for adventure and risk and the feminine urge for safe domesticity. At the same time, however, the film is clearly uncomfortable with its own solutions. At least a touch of irony, for example, surrounds Philip's wife, Jess, who is so domesticated, so positioned within a world of children and homemaking, as to be oblivious of the dangers her test-pilot husband undergoes. And yet Jess is clearly offered as a positive contrast to the constantly worrying Susan, who for her part yearns for the simple life Jess represents. Neither woman, significantly, truly understands what it is their men are doing. The only real difference between them is that one is comfortable with her incomprehension and the other is not. In short, one is attractively silly, the other unattractively neurotic. Lean's film reflects the social environment of the early 1950s. Women, to some degree emancipated by the conditions of war (when we first see Susan, she is in uniform—and for her wedding, no less!), were repositioned into traditional roles. Nineteen fifty-one marks both the return of Tory rule and the beginning of the so-called "Age of Affluence." The film, in any case, ends by suggesting that a peaceful and all-embracing domesticity allows for masculine achievement in a way that a potentially richer but less placid home life does not. Jess's husband breaks the sound barrier and survives; Susan's dies in the attempt.

A similar confusion surrounds the central issue of the worth of technological achievement weighted in terms of traditional values, including human life itself. The entire film is posed as a debate on this very issue, but the terms of the debate are either not clearly presented or are made irrelevant by the scenario's design. The argument on the side of technology, which the film ultimately validates, amounts to little more than semimystical pronouncements ("I believe we can force our way through this barrier . . . and once through . . . there is a world, a whole new world within the grasp of man") and non sequiturs ("What purpose did Scott have in going to the South Pole?"). Against this, we are given either blank incomprehension or *ad hominem* accusations that the film's fictional patterning shows to be unjust. Susan unfairly accuses her father of being an unfeeling man responsible for the deaths of both his son and his son-in-law, but he is neither unfeeling nor responsible, even though the film wants to suggest that he could very easily be both. The problem here is not that the film presents an unfair argument in favor of one or another point of view but that it presents arguments that cancel each other out while at the same time creating a dramatic fable that lands us squarely on one side of the issue.

At several moments in the film, the force of a more complex viewpoint insinuates itself just beneath the surface and even threatens to break through. In the sequence where Tony and Susan fly to Cairo for lunch, the film impresses us with the wonder of jet flight and with the insignificance of the world seen from a great height. During the last part of the sequence, Lean cuts in shots first of the Acropolis as they fly over Athens and then of the Sphinx as they prepare to land. Earlier, Susan had re-

Ralph Richardson and Ann Todd in The Sound Barrier.

marked that the earth was beginning to look awfully small and insignificant, to which Tony responded: "Down there's had it." But those shots of the Acropolis and the Sphinx, crumbling symbols of ancient, decayed civilization, actually give the lie to Tony's words. Mute observers to the plane flying overhead, their sheer physical beauty affirms the value of the past as it faces the future. Whatever Lean's intention here, the effect of the sequence is far more complex than any viewpoint the film as a whole can sustain. A similar effect arises from the characterization of Tony. As charmingly played by Nigel Patrick, Tony exhibits a boyishly romantic attitude toward flying. Even less capable than Ridgefield of articulating the significance of his work ("it's got to be done"; "Can't let the show down"), his whole ethos would seem to qualify the film's predominantly masculine values. As it turns out, however, it is not that Tony's values are wrong but rather that he is not intelligent enough (lacks the Right Stuff[4]) for the job at hand: "Tony hasn't got it up here," Ridgefield's chief designer says at one point; "that's what a pilot needs nowadays, brains and imagination." So Tony dies a hero's death, and his place is taken by someone with more brains and more imagination.

The film's characterization of Ridgefield reveals most clearly its central confusions. Ridgefield is an early, undeveloped manifestation of a character who will recur in later Lean films: Nicholson, Lawrence, and Strelnikov are all variations of the same conception, the visionary who sacrifices all to his vision. But unlike these later characters, Ridgefield is treated without irony. Lean takes him at face value, validating his vision, justifying all sacrifices. Whatever qualifications and criticisms Ridgefield's single-mindedness receives are deflected, neutralized, contained: they are not allowed to spill over into the consciousness of the viewer. Ralph Richardson's uncertain characterization suggests that neither he nor Lean and Rattigan ever quite decided what to make of John Ridgefield. Brilliant in a somewhat similar role in William Wyler's *The Heiress* several years earlier, Richardson here plays with a mannered, humorless, quirky emphasis. He gives, in fact, a frequently bad performance, self-conscious, unfocused, unsubtle. Ridgefield thus emerges as little more than a caricature who only infrequently engages us either intellectually or emotionally. The revelation that his monolithic exterior hides doubt, fear, and compassion lacks resonance since we never share or even perceive the force of his conflicting emotions. The sequence where he "sweats out" Phillip's flight in Susan's presence may be one of the least convincing scenes in a Lean film, a dramatic contraption in place of psychological credibility.

Susan, Ridgefield's only real antagonist, presents no coherent argument or concept to counterbalance his visionary spirit: she merely whines continually about not being able to understand. Her opposition is reduced to the "Feminine principle," the woman who cannot fathom what it is that men do until, in the end, she is brought around to accept, to acquiesce, not because she truly understands but because, finally, that is all a woman *can* do. When she learns that her father, beneath the hard exterior, has the "feminine" qualities of doubt, fear, and compassion, all is excused, all is forgiven. The real issues—the value of human life in relation to scientific progress, the meaning of technology, the impulse toward self-destruction—are never truly explored.

In the end, Lean and company may simply have boxed themselves in. In order to produce this film convincingly, they had to receive help from the very technological/industrial/scientific world they were investigating—in particular, the aircraft manufacturers de Havilland and Vickers, who provided the planes. Ridgefield represents—stands in for—the men who ran these companies. The film specifically alludes to the fatal 1946 crash of test pilot Geoffrey de Havilland, son of the firm's founder, Sir Geoffrey, who had earlier lost another son in an air accident. Under the circumstances, one may wonder how far Lean and Rattigan could have gone in questioning either the ethos of a man like Ridgefield or the value of supersonic flight. Within the film, of course, Ridgefield is criticized from several points of view; but he is not (could not be?) criticized *by* the film. Furthermore, the film celebrates (and distorts) British achievement at a time when Britain seemed to have precious few achievements to celebrate. Lean and Rattigan, after all, ignore the fact that an American, not an Englishman, first broke the sound barrier. A film that treads on such thin ground could hardly afford to indulge in irony.

While Lean worked on *The Sound Barrier*, the British people celebrated, in 1951, the Festival of Britain, which commemorated the centenary of the Great London Exhibition of 1851 with a South Bank fair and a variety of other activities. The British Film Institute contributed a special issue of *Sight and Sound* devoted to "Films in 1951." It may be some sign of Lean's shaky reputation with the British film establishment that not he but Carol Reed is featured in an article on "The Director." An essay in the same issue on "10 Years of British Films," written by Sir Michael Balcon, takes note of Lean's situation: "He has had recent setbacks, but his extraordinary singlemindedness and tenacity make me certain that he will survive these and again take his proper place as a director of international calibre."[5] These, as it turned out, were prophetic words; what Balcon did not foresee, however, was that, in the process, Lean would cease to be a British director except in name.

6

Going Hollywood

UP TO NOW, it has been possible as well as convenient to divide Lean's films into more or less cohesive groupings: four films associated with Noel Coward, two Dickens adaptations, three Ann Todd vehicles. The films now to be discussed do not lend themselves to such obvious categories. During the period covered by *Hobson's Choice*, *Summer Madness*, and *The Bridge on the River Kwai*, Lean became an international filmmaker, working in foreign, often exotic locales and financed, in whole or in part, by American money. He was absorbed, as was the British cinema, by Hollywood. His subjects ceased to be wholly British; his budgets grew astronomically; he spent more and more time on each film. By the time of *Dr. Zhivago* (1965), Lean had become one of the world's best-known and highest-paid directors. *Hobson's Choice* shows only a trace of the American connection, primarily in the presence of Charles Laughton, who, though British-born, had been a Hollywood star since the late 1930s. *Summer Madness* gestures much more clearly in Hollywood's direction: an American property, an American star (Katharine Hepburn), and a direct infusion of American money. *The Bridge on the River Kwai* completes the transformation. Only marginally a British film, it is Lean's first blockbuster epic and signals a new phase in his directorial career. He will make only three more films, each of epic size and cost. Two of these, *Lawrence of Arabia* and *Dr. Zhivago*, will be ranked among the most popular films of all time.

Hobson's Choice (1954)

Hobson's Choice, his only comedy other than *Blithe Spirit*, suggests that the comic muse may not be David Lean's most congenial partner. Not that *Hobson's Choice* fails to be funny. But Lean, by highlighting essentially noncomic themes and characters, isolates the humor in such a way that it becomes almost detachable, a decorative, eccentric flourish on an otherwise sober edifice. His mannered, detailed style turns the film into what might be described as a gothic comedy or baroque farce. As with his

Sessue Hayakawa and Alec Guinness in Bridge on the River Kwai.

Dickens adaptations—in particular, *Oliver Twist*—Lean borrows stylistically from German Expressionism, employing its elements to lend a patina of psychological sigificance to what started life as a slight portrait of English provincial life. A highly uneven film results, at once comic and grotesque, somber and lighthearted, psychologically compelling and yet filled with stock characters playing out stock situations.

On the evidence of his other films, one can guess that Lean was drawn to Harold Brighouse's popular play (already twice filmed, in 1920 and 1931) by the character of Maggie, the spinster daughter. Maggie fits easily into the gallery of Lean women whose need for love cannot be separated from a desire for independence, a strong sense of identity, and, perhaps most of all, self-respect. She may be the most fortunate of Lean heroines, however; unlike most of Lean's women, she inhabits an essentially comic world, which allows her to achieve both love and a strengthened sense of self. Indeed, she reaches all her goals at once, as each intrinsically connects to the others. Breaking away from her bullying father and an empty, dead-end life in his bootmaking establishment, Maggie wins financial independence, personal integrity, and, in marrying her father's skillful apprentice, Willie Mossip ("a business idea in the shape of a man," as she calls him) and setting up shop with him in rivalry to her father, the affection and respect of a good man. The conflict in *Hobson's Choice* is thus not internal, as it is in *The Passionate Friends* and *Summer Madness*, but external, daughter against father, and Lean from the outset leaves us little room to doubt the outcome. Maggie risks humiliation in courting the initially quite reluctant Willie, but the strength, dignity, and warmth of Brenda de Banzie's ideal performance forestalls any fear that she may stoop too far to conquer. Although at the center of a richly comic situation, she is an object of derision only to her father, and Hobson's misjudgment merely sweetens her all but inevitable victory. Willie, who is a bit thickheaded, struggles at first against Maggie's overwhelming presence but finally fits himself into her plans with scarcely a murmur of protest.

Harold Brighouse rooted his surprisingly charming and witty play ("surprisingly" because its critical reputation consigns it to the category of provincial repertory warhorses) firmly in its middle-class, late Victorian Lancashire setting. Lean's adaptation creates a lovingly detailed mise-en-scène that evokes, with great conviction, both period and milieu. The actual Lancashire locations, sparingly used throughout, harmonize unusually well with the studio sets. Lean renders the surface of things—wood and leather and cobblestoned streets—with conscious fidelity to the special beauty of skillfully made objects, of fine craftsmanship and quality materials. The film thus reinforces Brighouse's celebration of bourgeois values and middle-class achievements. *Hobson's Choice*, play and film, hearkens back to a strain of English fiction that runs from Chaucer's fablieaux to the mercantile myths of Defoe. In particular, one senses the at

Top: Charles Laughton, Brenda de Banzie, and John Mills in Hobson's Choice. *Bottom: Maggie (Brenda de Banzie) and her sisters in* Hobson's Choice.

least indirect influence of writers in the tradition of Thomas Deloney, who created middle-class fables from such humble material as the story of an upwardly mobile apprentice who marries the boss's widow. In all such fiction, evocative detail plays a crucial role: everyday objects must be presented with the care and awe that are given to crowns and swords and cloaks in a more exalted fictional tradition. In his opening sequence, for example, before any of the characters have been introduced, Lean's tracking camera lovingly caresses the rows of men's and women's shoes in Hobson's shop, establishing not only the film's setting but its tone and atmosphere as well.

Lean's fidelity to the spirit of Brighouse's play does not entirely succeed in absorbing Charles Laughton's larger-than-life, theatrical, barnstorming performance. Laughton turns Henry Hobson, drawn by Brighouse as a vivid but conventionally "heavy" father, into an incredible grotesque. Frequently resembling a beached whale, Laughton acts like an intruder from an entirely different story: King Lear, a role he would play in Stratford in 1959, has been suggested as a possibility. He indulges in every acting trick, every bit of mugging, every scene-stealing gesture or inflection at his disposal. Ignoring Brighouse's straightforward psychology, he raises a series of subtextual issues that never quite add up to a completely accessible characterization. Laughton fails to win sympathy for Hobson's predicament: Maggie and Willie remain—as they should—at the film's emotional center. And yet his performance, for all that, is fascinating to watch, the kind of grand, no-holds-barred "turn" that today rarely finds its way to the screen.

It may be that, as some critics have suggested, Lean was unable to control Laughton, always a difficult actor at best. And yet Lean clearly showcases and abets Laughton's interpretation, padding the role and even providing Laughton with bits of business that have no original in the play. Neither Lean nor Laughton allows Hobson to be merely funny; both reach instead for a pathos they do not quite achieve. Though the situations Hobson finds himself in may be comic, he is not a figure of fun: we laugh at but seldom with him. A petty and cruel domestic tyrant who bullies his daughters, beats his employees, ridicules his friends, and abases himself before his betters, Hobson embodies the dark side of both the Victorian parent and the Victorian employer. Lean and Laughton's attempt to humanize him actually backfires: his ultimate comeuppance—he ends up a defeated, beaten man—seems more than justified. The perfect Marxist embodiment of a capitalist, Hobson does no useful work (he spends all day in the local pub) while exploiting without hesitation the craftsmanship of his apprentice and the business talents of his daughter. Their rebellion thus has an economic as well as a moral and emotional logic.

Apart from the tone of Laughton's performance, there is evidence throughout *Hobson's Choice* that Lean wished to press Brighouse's rather slight play into directions it did not care to go, thus creating an imbalance between the significance of the fable on the one hand and stylistic expression on the other. The entire opening sequence, for example, seems in retrospect to belong to an altogether different film. Outside, the street is wet and dark, and a huge, boot-shaped sign sways and creaks in the wind. Inside Hobson's shop, boots and shoes seem to have a life of their own as the camera glides over them in the eerie half-light. The sound of a branch striking a window-pane motivates a quick pan to the window. The door flies open, the camera panning toward it, and a large shadow appears, followed by Hobson himself, drunk. Though beautifully done, the sequence seems finally somewhat ludicrous, so anticlimactic and overdetermined is Hobson's entrance. Lean's prologue does, however, prepare us for the discrepancies between motive and behavior in Laughton's performance. Perhaps he felt the need to set Laughton up by immediately evoking the world of the irrational and bizarre. The effect, in any case, seems studied and self-conscious.

A very thin line separates careful structuring from overcalculation, and Lean's direction in *Hobson's Choice* often balances on that line. In the tour-de-force sequence when the drunken Hobson chases the moon's reflection—which disappears from sight as soon as he comes near it—from rain puddle to rain puddle, the joke depends on the camera adopting Hobson's point of view: the technique manifests itself quite overtly without necessarily spoiling the humor, which has a dark, surrealistic tone. If we do not laugh wholeheartedly, it is in part because Hobson seldom inspires an unmixed response. Similarly, Hobson's bout with *delirium tremens*, in the course of which he and we see a gigantic flying insect and a huge mouse near his bed, is more grotesque than funny, more a grim temperance lesson than a joke. That these moments do not cross the line into mere academicism results from the integration of Lean's style with Laughton's performance. But when Laughton is not present, as with Willie Mossip's uncomfortably elaborate wedding-night preparations (complete with martial music, as if going to bed with Maggie were the supreme wartime sacrifice), Lean's studied approach to humor has less justification: an otherwise touching and genuine moment verges on embarrassing caricature.

However distracting some of Lean's stylistic quirks may occasionally be, the interaction between Brenda de Banzie's Maggie and John Mills's Willie Mossip continues to provide *Hobson's Choice* with a rich and genuine center of gravity. Mills, who took over the role from an ailing Robert Donat, has seldom been better. Considerably aided by a drolly appropriate haircut, he convincingly blends simplemindedness with integrity, subtly enacting the gradual process by which Willie, under Maggie's tutelage, becomes aware of himself as an independent, self-respecting human being. What begins as a business arrangement ends up as an emotional partnership, a process presented without coyness or sentimentality. Even those moments that depend to some extent on stereotypical responses to the dominating female—Maggie has to bully Willie into standing up for himself—are played in such a way that they become a positive force, part of Maggie's strategy for raising Willie's class consciousness and hence his self-respect. And, finally, it is Maggie, not Hobson, whose actions and desires provide the film with its structure and theme: both Hobson and Laughton end up outwitted and outmaneuvered by Brenda de Banzie's magnificent Maggie.

Summer Madness (1955)

Although *Summer Madness* (*Summertime* in the United States) moves Lean closer to Hollywood, it remains very much a David Lean film, hearkening back to the themes and situations of *Brief Encounter*. In adapting Arthur Laurents's play *The Time of the Cuckoo*, Lean and H. E. Bates remain faithful to the narrative outline of their source while radically transforming its thematic and emotional center. Laurents's play delineates in a none-too-subtle fashion the conflicting cultural and emotional values of an American spinster, Leona Samish (Jane Hudson in the film),and the city of Venice, with all that it represents in terms of Italian morals and manners. A woman who hides a yearning for romance behind quick jokes and an easy affability, Leona is presented as typically American in her lack of spontaneity and her material interpretation of human relations. Courted by an attractive, middle-aged, married, poor Italian shopkeeper, Leona, though she enters into the excitement of it all, finds romance disappointing and cannot quite free herself from suspecting her lover's motives, suspicions to some degree justified. The romance ends almost as soon as it begins, and Leona, disillusioned but not entirely crushed by her experience, returns to America.

Though this summary could, with a few modifications, serve as a description of the film, it would be a distortion of it. In *Summer Madness*, Jane Hudson (Katharine Hepburn) puts aside her suspicions and gives herself wholly to a passionate love affair. The Italian, Di Rossi (Rossano Brazzi), a much more plausible lover here than in the play, is swept up as well. The affair ends not because the lovers cannot trust each other but because Jane, knowing the situation to be impossible and fearful that her feelings will totally sway her judgment, wills that it must. The play stresses the cultural differences between Americans and Italians: Americans worry too much, especially about matters of the heart and the libido; Italians do not worry enough. Lean shifts the emphasis toward the theme of romantic yearning in conflict with social reality, expressed in *Brief Encounter* and *The Passionate Friends* and to be taken up again in *Doctor Zhivago* and *Ryan's Daughter*. The film, as a result, is a more poignant, if less acerbic, treatment of romance than the play.

Summer Madness gives us something else that *Time of the Cuckoo* cannot, except by implication: Venice. Lean's first film to be shot entirely outside England, *Summer Madness* exploits—some would say overexploits—its exotic setting. Venice has probably never looked better on film than it does here, nor has its spirit been captured so convincingly. If Lean at times indulges in pictorialism, he has the excuse of his heroine's ever-present home movie camera. Our view of Venice is her view, and her view is through the lens of a Bolex. The Venice of *Summer Madness* undeniably belongs to tourists, existing to be seen, not to be inhabited. At the same time, the self-consciousness with which Jack Hildyard's camera records, in muted, autumnal colors, the monuments and sights of this magnificent Renaissance city identifies *Summer Madness* as a 1950s location film, one of the many, particularly American, films of the period to be shot in picturesque places, especially Italy (*Roman Holiday* [William Wyler, 1953] and *Three Coins in the Fountain* [Jean Negulesco, 1954], among others). As an example of the "travelogue" genre, *Summer Madness* has a very different look from location films made after the magic had worn off. Another British filmmaker, Nicholas Roeg, shows us a far less congenial Venice in *Don't Look Now* (1973), a compendium of threatening and sinister images. The picture-postcard loveliness of *Summer Madness* hearkens back to an era when a favorable exchange rate contributed to a burgeoning American tourism.

The Venetian cityscape, however, serves as much more than a backdrop to the action. Photographed in slightly melancholy, Turneresque tones, Venice contributes a heightened, overripe atmosphere, a twilight world of dawns and sunsets, that both feeds and threatens Jane Hudson's hope for romance. Like this most unreal, magical of cities, Jane's love affair, literally a madness, exists only in suspended time, cut off physically as well as temporally from the world outside. Jane's arrival to and departure from Venice frames *Summer Madness*; her life before and after are blanks. The film script, like the play, provides few specifics of Jane's everyday life in America. She vaguely refers to her job (a "fancy secretary") and also to a married couple who seem to be her only friends: otherwise, nothing. Jane's trip to Venice thus encapsulates her life, and her response to it provides us with the only touchstone we have to the private longings of this middle-aged virgin from Akron, Ohio.

The Venetian setting also helps to disguise how much the character of Jane Hudson approaches the borders of cliché. The dried-up spinster seeking romance may be one of the more embarrassing relics of the 1950s; Jane Hudson's situation dates the film as certainly as do her clothes. So, too, does her sexual prudery, not because a woman in her situation would not be a prude but because so much is made of her prudishness to no significant end. A middle-aged virgin need not seem foolish; if Jane, at times, does, it is because she (and, by implication, any middle-aged woman) so desperately wants not to be a virgin, because her virginity is seemingly not a matter of choice but of circumstance.[1]

Katharine Hepburn adroitly skirts many of the dangers inherent in Jane Hudson as a character, but even she cannot quite transmute the conventionalities of the role without at the same time undermining the film's credibility. Her performance in *Summer Madness*, beautifully tempered as it frequently is, reveals some of the difficulties a distinctive female star faced in adjusting to middle age in the 1950s. In 1955, Hepburn was forty-six; at that age, male stars like Cary Grant or Clark Gable continued to be romantic leading men. (On the other hand, Spencer Tracy made few good films in his mid-forties, while actors like Henry Fonda and James Stewart worked successfully into middle age because they were always more character actors than leading men; the problem was not endemic to women, but more seriously affected their careers.) The decade started well enough for Hepburn with such films as *The African Queen* and *Pat and Mike* (both 1952), but much of her subsequent work was unfortunate (*The Iron Petticoat* [1956]; *The Rainmaker* [1956]; *Suddenly Last Summer* [1959]), presenting her either with roles that worked against the grain of her personality or encouraged her most theatrical mannerisms. As Jane Hudson, Hepburn is both perfect and perfectly wrong. Perfect because her screen persona—her always-evident independence and strength of character—works against the pathos of Jane's predicament. Perfectly wrong because she seems unable or unwilling to draw the necessary elements of Jane's character out of herself. As she often does with uncongenial roles, Hepburn occasionally miscalculates her effects. (One of cinema's finest actresses, she can also be one of its most irritating: witness such films as *Morning Glory* [1933], *Mary of Scotland* [1936], and *The Rainmaker.*) She is often shrill when she should be high-strung, angry when she should be hurt, aggressive when she should be defensive.

On balance, however, Hepburn gives a skillful and frequently moving performance in *Summer Madness*, and even the wrong notes can be seen as a critique of the role from within. She is at her best in the early, reflective sequences. Lean and Hepburn perfectly capture Jane's yearning—her need for a miracle that will take her out of herself—in the scene where Jane has been left alone at her *pensione*. On the soundtrack, a highly romantic theme. A breeze lightly disturbs the evening stillness. Jane strolls across the balcony, her steps firm but purposeless, her casual manner holding in check her nervous energy and mounting pain. She hears a burst of girlish laughter and then, as Lean cuts from a medium to a medium-close shot on Hepburn's turn toward the camera, we see her barely suppressed tears. Hepburn projects the inner resources, the good sense and straightforward approach to nonsexual matters that lend the character sympathy and forestall pity. Few actresses could deliver the line "I'm the

Katharine Hepburn in Summer Madness.

independent type—always have been" with such conviction: her entire film career resonates in those words. In her scenes with the street urchin, in particular, Hepburn's openness and humor lend credence to an otherwise unlikely relationship. Clearly a woman unsentimental about children, she treats the boy like an adult, rejecting the cuteness and sentimentality inherent in the situation. And as a lover, Hepburn is totally credible and touching; never coy even when given coy things to say; always frank and open.

Lean's direction, like Hepburn's performance, maintains a sometimes uneasy balance between pathos and detachment. His austere use of space and minimal editing provides an understated mise-en-scène that holds the heightened emotionalism of the plot at a distance. He photographs many scenes in a single take and even the intimate conversations between Jane and di Rossi are mostly two-shots: *Summer Madness* contains few individual close-ups or reaction shots. Some of this visual austerity may admittedly owe something to location filming. Jane's encounter with the American couple on the *vaperetto,* for instance, was very likely shot in one take because it would have been difficult and time-consuming to do otherwise (although such challenges do not normally deter Lean): there are only so many places you can position a camera on a moving boat and, of course, any new camera set up would require a repetition of some part of the journey, problems that can be ignored in studio filming. In other, less constrained situations, Lean may not have wanted to sacrifice the pictorial integrity of the Venetian cityscape by breaking it up with a variety of camera placements. External considerations aside, Lean's unadorned style provides a "cool" structure that objectifies Jane Hudson's experience. Even the music, which features a lovely, poignant melody by Alessandro Cicognini, is, like the Rachmaninoff concerto in *Brief Encounter,* both ambient and nonambient, simultaneously objective and subjective. First heard at the café where Jane and di Rossi dance, later played (at di Rossi's request) by the band in the Piazza San Marco, it becomes an irrational expression of Jane's love affair. Even the remarkably beautiful, self-consciously "pictorial" sequence of shots that summarize the moments of romantic ecstasy are double-edged: the sunrises and sunsets, the fireworks bursting in the night sky, capture the intensity but also foreshadow the briefness of this love affair. If we never become entirely swept away by Jane Hudson's romantic experience, it is in part because of Lean's stylistic self-restraint, the fine balance between engagement and detachment that he maintains throughout.

Summer Madness, like *Brief Encounter,* like *Madeleine,* like *The Passionate Friends,* places a woman's consciousness, and a woman's will, at the center of the text. Like the heroines of these earlier films, Jane Hudson briefly experiences the anguish and joy of a transcendent romantic experience before returning to an unromantic reality. And, like Lean's earlier women in love, she survives the experience with dignity and grace. Initially a neurotic virgin surrounded and intimidated by sexually "normal" people (the young American couple at the *pensione,* the earthy Italian widow), Jane by the end of the film reverses the clichés that initially form her character and reveals herself as stronger, wiser, and more realistic than the man she loves (as well as those other "normal" people). It is she who breaks off the affair (in the play, di Rossi made the final decision) and, as her train leaves Venice, it is he who must run after her. In contrast to most romantic films, particularly of the 1950s, the man's need and the man's pain seem greater than the woman's. *Summer Madness* ends by focusing not on Jane's pain, which is unquestionably real, but on her point of view, her gaze, which controls the ever-receding image of the lover she has rejected.

In a generally dreary year for both British and American films, *Summer Madness* was something of a highlight. Lean and Hepburn were nominated for "Oscars" in their respective categories, and Lean received the New York Film Critics Award for best direction. The film did not help Alexander Korda, however, whose distribution company, British Lion, went bankrupt. The failure of British Lion coincided with and contributed to the beginning of a new phase in the history of British films and in David Lean's career. The year 1955 saw a dramatic expansion in television ownership among the British working classes, and, as John Sproas has shown, "each new set dealt a heavy blow to the cinema."[2] Movie theaters began to close at an ever-increasing rate. At the same time, more and more American films were being made in Britain. Hollywood could benefit from lower labor costs while spending its blocked earnings and, by qualifying as "British" under the quota system, profiting from the levy on admissions in aid of British films. Hollywood was also recruiting British directors. Carol Reed made *Trapeze* for Columbia with Burt Lancaster and Tony Curtis, while Alexander Mackendrick, formerly one of Ealing Studios' top directors, guided the same two stars in *Sweet Smell of Success*. David Lean joined the exodus. Soon after the release of *Summer Madness*, he was hired by the American producer Sam Spiegel to direct *The Bridge on the River Kwai*. Although Spiegel's production company, Horizon Pictures, was registered in Great Britain, his financial backing came primarily from Columbia.

The Bridge on the River Kwai (1957)

Lean now turned his back completely on the relatively cozy, self-contained, financially modest world of British films and entered the large-scale, big-budget arena of international coproduction. When *The Bridge on the River Kwai* premiered at London's Plaza Theatre, the front-of-the-house display hailed it as "A British Achievement to Stand for All Time." The realities of film financing and distribution in the 1950s tell a different story, however. Quite simply, the British film industry could not have made a film of this scope and cost without American help. And American money, of course, meant a large American presence. Carl Foreman and Michael Wilson, two blacklisted American expatriates, helped shape the screenplay. Columbia cast William Holden, one of Hollywood's most popular male stars, in a leading role written especially for him and gave him top billing over the film's two British leads, Alec Guinness and Jack Hawkins. In large and small ways, *The Bridge on the River Kwai*, both as a material construct and in its thematic concerns, evidences various signs of this American connection.

Carl Foreman, from whom Sam Spiegel purchased the rights to Pierre Boulle's 1954 novel, wrote a first-draft screenplay featuring an invented American commando and beginning with a lengthy episode unconnected to the central prison-camp plot. In quite a number of ways, Foreman's script differs considerably both from Boulle's novel and from the released film; even Boulle's protagonist, the British Colonel Nicholson, becomes a secondary character in this initial treatment (which may explain why Alec Guinness at first turned down the role). Foreman's work on the film, in any case, seems to have ended with this first draft; given the opportunity to clear himself with HUAC, he returned to the United States. Michael Wilson, hired to write a second draft, continued the process of building up the American character and may also have helped to bring the film into greater congruence with Boulle's original structure. Whatever the precise nature of their contribution, neither Foreman nor Wilson received screen credit. Pierre Boulle, who was quick to admit that he had not actually written any of the dialogue, is listed as sole author. Since Lean nearly always worked on the scripts of his films (as, to some extent, did Spiegel), usually without credit, it is virtually impossible to determine who "really" wrote the movie. At the time, neither Foreman nor Wilson was in any position to discuss the matter too loudly; later, they would claim to have been cheated of both a credit and an Oscar.

In light of this admittedly hazy history, one might at least expect the film to exhibit a left-leaning, American viewpoint. Actually, there is very little of this in Foreman's draft screenplay.[3] A few traces of such an attitude can be found primarily in the dialogue created for the American, Shears, much of which was probably written by Michael Wilson. In truth, however, Boulle's novel is sufficiently ironic in tone to make room for much of what Shears has to say. The film as released projects an amalgam of French, British, and American attitudes engaged in a debate on topics not always clearly defined or articulated. *The Bridge on the River Kwai* becomes a stage on which certain abstractions—heroism, pride, class, "face," hierarchy, will, power—perform a morality play with no clear moral. Lean's direction, in its objectivity and detachment, allows conflicting viewpoints to speak for themselves, establishing an ironic, ambivalent tone that pervades all aspects of the film.

The film's various thematic strands can be detected even in a brief summary of its plot, which, at least in outline, follows Boulle's novel quite closely. The setting is a Japanese prisoner-of-war camp in Siam soon after the fall of Singapore. The camp commander, Colonel Saito, has been ordered to build a stretch of railroad and a bridge to carry it across the Kwai

River. The ranking British POW, Colonel Nicholson, rejects Saito's demand that officers perform manual labor, arguing that this contravenes provisions of the Geneva Convention. Severely punished, Nicholson refuses to break down. It is Saito, finally, who, unable to build the bridge without Nicholson's cooperation, must give in. Nicholson regains command of his troops and, partly to promote morale among the prisoners and partly to teach the Japanese a lesson in Western methods, proceeds to build a better bridge than the Japanese could have built for themselves. In the meantime, however, a British commando squad is parachuted into the jungle with orders to blow up the bridge upon its completion. The commandos succeed in mining the bridge but, at the last moment, Nicholson discovers the preparations (without quite understanding their significance) and, his pride in his handiwork subsuming other considerations, tries to prevent the commandos from carrying out their mission. In the ensuing melee, Nicholson, Saito, and two of the three commandos are killed.

The above plot summary, intentionally worded so as to stress similarities, suppresses the differences between Boulle's novel and Lean's film. The novel, with its lightly sketched characters, its ironic tone, and its carefully balanced structure, reads very much like a fable or philosophical tale. Fascinated by the varying responses of different men to the same stimuli, Boulle creates characters who imprison themselves within rigid concepts. He takes obvious Gallic relish in dissecting British behavior. All of these Englishmen are more or less foolish, though one cannot help respecting their courage, ingenuity, and commitment to principle. While Lean adopts aspects of Boulle's ironic tone, particularly in his attitudes toward Colonel Nicholson, he does not produce nearly as schematic a text. Lean's ending, for example, significantly alters Boulle's thematic intentions. In the film, Nicholson recognizes his error at the last moment and, fatally wounded, collapses on the detonator, destroying the bridge; in the novel, the bridge remains intact. Of perhaps more significance thematically, one of Boulle's secondary British characters, Shears, becomes an American in the film, a sea-change that has large consequences. Promoted to the status of a major character, Shears (William Holden) escapes from Saito's prison camp early in the film, later returning as a member of the British commando unit. The "outsider" point of view, the tone of generalized cynicism and American "common sense" he introduces into the film text, is quite unlike anything in the novel, where only the medical officer, Clipton, can be said to represent, from time to time, a viewpoint parallel to, but not necessarily congruent with, the author's.

Lean's tone, more subtle and more ambivalent than Boulle's, emerges clearly in his characterization of the Japanese commandant, Saito. Although not as grossly stereotyped as in the novel, where Boulle presents him as a chronic, hysterical drunk, a "grotesque figure . . . [whose] head wobbled on his shoulders like a puppet's,"[4] Sessue Hayakawa's Saito nevertheless balances uneasily between caricature and character. If at times he speaks like a veteran of wartime Hollywood—"I spent three years in London, you know, I studied at the London Polytechnic"—he can also rise to genuine and heartfelt eloquence, responding with a measured outburst to Nicholson's maddening *sangfroid*: "I hate the British—you are defeated, but you have no shame; you are stubborn, but you have no pride; you endure, but you have no courage." At other times, Saito behaves like a parody of Westerners, dining on corned beef, drinking Johnny Walker Red ("I prefer it to saki"), smoking cigars, and keeping an American pin-up calendar ("Joey's Garage, Elk City, Ohio") on his wall: the perfect, imitative Japanese. Yet Lean stresses, far more than does the novel, the extent to which Saito is, in many ways, the counterpart to Nicholson. He, too, is a man molded by military tradition, guided by an inflexible code, supremely egotistical, instinctively imperialistic. The dignified sense of ritual and the subtle hint of ultimate vulnerability Sessue Hayakawa invests in the role insures that Saito never entirely descends into the world of simple stereotype. Indeed, Hayakawa makes Saito, who in frustration becomes alternately severe and ingratiating ("All work and no play make Jack a dull boy"), in his own way sympathetic, thereby complicating our response to Nicholson's exhilarating victory over him.

The casting of Alec Guinness as Nicholson and William Holden as Shears further contributes to the film's ambiguity and complexity. Alec Guinness, in 1957, presented an unpredictable quality to an international film audience. Outside the British Isles, especially, Guinness was known primarily, where he was known at all, as a comic actor, the star of several very popular Ealing comedies of the early 1950s. More perceptive filmgoers would perhaps remember him from *Great Expectations* and *Oliver Twist*. Guinness had no clearly recognizable screen persona (in one of his most popular films, *Kind Hearts and Coronets* [1949], he played eight characters). In *Bridge on the River Kwai*, therefore, Colonel Nicholson, too, is initially an unknown quantity about whom we have to learn, from moment to moment, in the course of the film. He remains ambiguous to the very end. William Holden, on the other hand, presents the opposite phenomenon, a well-known international star with a familiar screen persona—the shallow, handsome cynic—developed in the early 1950s. Even before Shears/Holden speaks, we know what he is going to say. Indeed, so familiar are we with the actor and the role that we initially take both for granted. The cynical antihero seems an unpromising stereotype, and the first third, at least, of the film does not credit his viewpoint. It is only when we begin to see the folly of Nicholson that we are encouraged to reconsider Shear's cynicism.

In Colonel Nicholson we have the archetypal Lean protagonist: the fanatic who attempts to impose his inflexible sense of destiny on the world around him. Of iron courage and fixed vision, he refuses to accept human limitations, his own or anyone else's. T. E. Lawrence and Pasha Antipov will follow in the Nicholson mold; Ridgefield has preceded him. Initially, Nicholson merely seems the embodiment of the stiff-upper-lip British soldier, an admirable—if slightly ludicrous—stereotype hearkening back to Captain "D" in *In Which We Serve*. Lean builds the first third of the film to the exhilarating moment of Nicholson's victory over Saito. Lean's brilliant use of the insidiously rousing "Colonel Bogey March," which is whistled defiantly by the British POWs, contributes greatly to the audience's emotional involvement with Nicholson's courage and tenacity. All at once, however, our admiration turns to dismay: blind to the consequences, Nicholson proceeds to build the Japanese their bridge and thus to demonstrate the superiority of British discipline and know-how. The hero has become a madman. From this point on, Shears's attitude not only begins to seem more sensible but morally preferable as well. But our response to Nicholson is further complicated both by certain humanizing details in the script and even more by the subtle intelligence of Alec Guinness's performance. So well does Guinness fill in the lines of Nicholson's character that we are constantly caught between admiration and exasperation. The admiration may, of course, be as much for Guinness as for Nicholson, and yet Guinness is so self-effacing an actor, so capable in his best performances of getting inside the skin of the character he plays, that we cannot easily separate the two. The actor is completely absorbed by the character.

With William Holden, the effect is just the reverse: the character is absorbed by the actor. Holden's role in *Kwai* is very much like America's role in the British film industry: an intrusive, superior, condescending, brash, "know it all" presence. Amused and disgusted by British ways, seemingly uncommitted to any ideals higher than his own survival and detached from any sense of common effort or common goal, Shears/Holden, by the end of the film, becomes the spokesman for an uncomplicated, nonideological humanism. "The only important thing," he ringingly asserts, "is how to live like a human being." Living like a human being is, of course, never defined. In the end, like other antiheroes before him, Shears gets caught up in the mission he has ridiculed and dies trying to save it. Along the way, however, he speaks very much like a 1957—not a 1943—humanist. "I don't care about your bridge," he says at one point, and he might as well be saying, "I don't care about your war." That no one says to him, "It's your bridge/war, too, Yank," or at least, "Remember Pearl Harbor," emphasizes the film's willingness to slight its own historical context. As in other prisoner-of-war films made in peacetime (most notably, Jean Renoir's *La Grande Illusion*, 1937), the war itself seems almost an irrelevance. Holden's separate peace, in any case, has a certain logic to it: in this part of the world, anyway, it *is* Britain's war, a war for the preservation of the British Empire. The Japanese are building a railroad that will give them a route to India, as Major Warden (Jack Hawkins) notes. Although the point is not stressed, it adds to the irony of Nicholson's position. A regular officer, his service in India, as he tells Saito in a rare moment of personal reflection, has given him his happiest years.

Lean's film has been criticized for "its refusal to take any stand outside the consciousness of its characters,"[5] a judgment that seems to ignore matters of style entirely. The script, admittedly, does not encourage us to equate any single viewpoint with the director's own. The medical officer, Clipton (James Donald), who speaks the film's final words—"Madness, madness"—serves as a kind of Greek chorus, which is not quite the same thing. *The Bridge on the River Kwai*, as we have seen, juxtaposes varying points of view, playing characters and situations off each other, suggesting similarities where differences are expected. The structure of the film and the local editing strategies reflect this, as does the composition of the individual CinemaScope frames. In effect, the absence of an explicit external viewpoint becomes itself a judgment on the characters and actions. The main title sequence announces and prefigures the tone of ironic distance Lean will maintain throughout. The first shot reveals a hawk circling in the sky in lyrical close-up; Lean cuts to a long shot of the mountains from the bird's (putative) point of view; in the third shot, the camera cranes down from treetop level, through the jungle underbrush, to reveal a row of wooden crosses next to a railway track. All that we subsequently experience, both of heroism and of folly, will be qualified by the suggestive structuring of these opening shots.

Lean shows himself adept and ingenious (though not quite as imaginative as he will be in *Lawrence of Arabia*) in this his first employment of the wide-screen image, which both elongates and deepens filmic space. (All of Lean's previous films involved composing for an image with a width to height ratio of 1.33:1; the CinemaScope image has a ratio of 2.55:1.) In particular, he effectively "edits within the shot," positioning a figure on one side of the image in close-up while a figure on the other side will be in medium or long shot, one or both of whom will move closer to or farther away from the image plane during the shot. The conversation between Nicholson and Shears in the medical hut, which is witnessed by Clipton, illustrates this approach. Composition and movement chart the relationship between the men and help to delineate their individual qualities. Shears, feigning sickness, lies on a cot foreground left; Nicholson, in medium and medium long-shot on the right, walks around the hut, a model of military bearing and cool detachment; Clipton, the mediating figure, stands in the middle, not quite understanding either man. Even a brief, static shot can have the effect of summarizing psychological dynamics. Notable in this respect is the moment in Saito's hut that foreshadows Nicholson's total victory. Nicholson, frame left, bends over, hands on knees, examining Saito's model of the bridge, placed on a table frame right. Saito sits in between, but in the background of the frame. From now on, the composition tells us, only Nicholson and the bridge matter; Saito is irrelevant.

The Bridge on the River Kwai is marked by a more strictly classical formalism than is usual with Lean. There is very little here of the baroque or expressionist tendencies evident in earlier—and to be evident in later—films. The primary structural devices are balance and antithesis, the film consisting of sequences that alternate between the prison camp and the commando squad. As the climax approaches, the narrative units become shorter and shorter, diminishing in length and narrowing in content from sequence to scene to shot. In the moments before the bridge explodes, the editing has become so frenetic as to confuse some viewers. But what confusion there is—in fact very little; Lean creates the illusion of confusion—is certainly deliberate. Throughout the film, we have been watching men plan, organize, and build. Both constructing the bridge and plotting its destruction are complex, carefully structured operations. And both of these well-laid plans end in chaos and blood; nothing goes as planned; rationalism, in this military context, is shown to be bankrupt. The film, too, careful and deliberate in its exposition and development, ends at the moment of climax. What makes *Kwai* particularly powerful is that Lean does not linger over the denouement. There is no postmortem, no clarification or explanation. The camera pulls up and away from the ruined bridge and dead men, and the final image of a hawk circling in the peaceful sky takes us back to the beginning, to the world of nature and to a viewpoint from which all human effort must appear equally foolish.

Throughout *The Bridge on the River Kwai*, Lean returns to the mode of his opening and closing shots, frequently employing high camera angles whose recurrence reminds us of a viewpoint external to the immediate concerns of particular individuals. Even, and especially, highly charged moments are photographed from a distance, both physical and emotional. When Nicholson is taken into the hut to be beaten by Japanese guards, the camera remains outside; when he emerges soon afterwards and is dragged off to the "oven," Lean keeps him in long shot. A long shot can also stress an ironic point, as when the commando unit watches, from a great distance, as Nicholson kneels down on the bridge next to a Japanese officer. The commandos assume he is being verbally and physically abused; actually, he is putting the finishing touches on a plaque commemorating the building of the bridge. Such a "bird's eye" view can reduce human beings to geometric patterns, but it can also impose momentary

Colonel Nicholson's moment of truth in Bridge on the River Kwai.

order on a seemingly chaotic world, as in the striking shot that includes Nicholson and his officers standing at attention as the work detail of enlisted men returns to camp at dusk. Here the artist and Nicholson are one: just as Nicholson maintains order among his troops by holding fast to the rigid details of military discipline, so Lean contains all turmoil within a beautifully composed frame of lines and points, all evenly bathed in the soft, tranquil light of a dying day.

Lean's visual strategies ultimately converge to emphasize the film's true subject and "star": the bridge itself. Unlike many "epic" films, *The Bridge on the River Kwai* justifies its length and size by involving us in a truly epic task: the building of an aesthetically pleasing and structurally sound bridge employing only the men, materials, and makeshift technology to be found in a primitive and forbidding jungle. The scope of the film, as well as the "scope" of the image (specifically, CinemaScope), lends in turn an epic dimension to the building of the bridge. On one level of expression, it is therefore part of the film's project to convince us that this bridge is a "real" bridge; not, that is, a model, or a painting on glass, or any other kind of substitution for a real bridge of a certain size and weight constructed of certain materials. Lean convinces us of the bridge's reality by

The Bridge on the River Kwai.

employing codes that are inconsistent with those we associate with special effects and fakery: he films the bridge from different angles; he varies the distance between the bridge and the camera; he tracks along the bridge; he shows recognizably human figures on and next to the bridge; and so forth. All of this may seem unremarkable enough, a mere by-product of the striving for realism, but within the context established by the film's plot and theme as well as the larger context of social, political, and economic forces that impinge on the film, it becomes particularly crucial that the bridge be credible and impressive, that it reflect the craft and expense put into it; and that it signify, as well, the craft and expense put into the film that contains it.

The Bridge on the River Kwai clearly celebrates Western technology and know-how, but this celebration, at least in retrospect, is deeply ironic. The British build the Japanese a bridge on the assumption, which the film pretty much endorses, that the Japanese are incapable of building it themselves. The bridge, however, contributes to the Japanese war effort against the British. So the British, with the help of an American, destroy the bridge they have built. It was still possible, in the mid-1950s, to assert the superiority of Western technology: after all, only cheap goods were then appearing in the West marked "Made in Japan"; the cameras, stereos, and television sets were still to come. But it is late enough to see the ironies inherent in that assertion of superiority. Slightly more than a month after David Lean and his crew began filming in Ceylon, an event occurred that brings into focus the underlying implications of *The Bridge on the River Kwai.* On 5 November 1956, English and French paratroopers landed at Port Said. Earlier in the year, Colonel Nasser had nationalized the Suez Canal Company. According to historians Alan Sked and Chris Cook, all shades of British political opinion "demanded that [Prime Minister Sir Anthony] Eden should stand no nonsense from this Arab guttersnipe."[6] The British-French (and Israeli) action, however, was a political fiasco. The United States, which, in the person of John Foster Dulles, may have assured the British of at least tacit support, immediately condemned their allies in the United Nations, where a cease-fire was called for. Lacking at least passive American support, and threatened by possible Soviet intervention, the Europeans were forced to withdraw. With the Suez affair, "Britain . . . served notice to the world that she was no longer a great power."[7]

Parallels between the Suez debacle and Lean's film are not hard to find. The canal, like the bridge, was a monument to Western technology threatening to serve non-Western interests. The underlying assumptions behind British action in Egypt—that Nasser was a petty dictator unworthy of respect; that the Egyptians were not capable of running the canal; that Europeans possess a moral and intellectual superiority to dark-skinned peoples that justifies any kind of high-handed behavior—are similar to Colonel Nicholson's assumptions about the Japanese. Even the American role is similar in both instances. Fancifully, we might see Nicholson as Anthony Eden and Shears as John Foster Dulles. Nicholson wants to preserve the image of British superiority at even suicidal cost; Shears, ostensibly an ally but actually a cynical bystander, helps to deliver the coup de grace to Nicholson's plan. Nicholson's intransigence, his ultimate folly, has nevertheless a heroic component to it; Shears's cheap cynicism seems opportunistic by contrast. Nicholson, at least, is building something and simultaneously upholding what he considers to be British honor. Shears can only destroy.

The visual "presence" and tangible reality of Colonel Nicholson's bridge is additionally significant in a manner that points to an obvious but important difference between film and literature. Both in the novel and in the film, the bridge represents the human need to "make," to create even in the midst of chaos. But Lean's bridge, engineered by Husband and Company, Sheffield, and constructed by Equipment and Construction Company, Ceylon (as the credits proudly inform us), is at once a technical wonder and a pleasing aesthetic object, and we experience it as such. Ian Watt, in a very useful essay on both the novel and the film that draws on his experience as a prisoner of war in Burma, considered it a flaw in Lean's film that it "seemed to have been conceived in terms of pictures that would justify the splendor of its technical equipment":

> One's most lasting impression was of the bridge itself with its two great cantilevers whose shape and color were in such perfect harmony with the surrounding landscape: it was a bridge whose poised serenity made credible, if anything could, Colonel Nicholson's infatuation with it as a symbol of permanent human achievement, but it was not a bridge that could possibly have been constructed without much greater material resources than would have been available under the conditions of the story.[8]

Although Watt nicely summarizes the bridge's effect, and though his objection may be valid from a purely technical consideration, he shows little understanding of cinematic stylization. That the bridge should be grander than anything we could reasonably expect is, after all, the point. It is in some sense miraculous, a technological marvel, a symbol of what British know-how, backed by American dollars, can accomplish. Lean's film, which includes the bridge, is also included in it; the film, like the bridge, was constructed at great expense and with great ingenuity in the inhospitable jungles of the Far East.

In the novel, as noted, the bridge is not destroyed. Its destruction in the film has been seen, by Watt and others, as a concession to Hollywood values that undercuts the novel's irony. The idea, presumably, is that the bridge had to be blown up in order not to disappoint audience expectations. Commercial calculation no doubt played a role, and no one would deny that to build a quarter-million-dollar bridge and then destroy it may be the ultimate in Hollywood-style conspicuous consumption. But the irony, it seems to me, is not diminished thereby but increased. We may remember, since we have been told, that the destruction of the bridge is necessary to the war effort, but within the context established by the film this remains a secondary consideration. The war effort, as I have already suggested, is marginal to the film's concerns. Had *The Bridge on the River Kwai* been released in 1943 rather than 1957, the effect would be quite different. As it is, we are caught up in a drama of a different kind. The construction of the last part of the film, the cross-cutting among Nicholson, Warden, Shears, and the young commando, Joyce, creates an emotional desire to see the bridge blown up, certainly. But the actual explosion is not cathartic. The bridge was a satisfying aesthetic object, and whatever pleasure we may derive from watching it collapse is not unmixed with a sense of loss. Within a context that shines an ironic light on nearly all values men fight and die for, only aesthetics seem redeemable. The destruction of the bridge thus becomes the film's final and greatest irony; the film itself quickly self-destructs: all is vanity.

7

Lawrence of Arabia (1962)

RELEASED TO critical acclaim, *The Bridge on the River Kwai* achieved enormous popular success and went on to win seven Academy Awards, including best film, best actor (Alec Guinness), and best director. Spiegel and Lean had every reason to continue their partnership. But Lean did not hurry into a new project; his pace was, as usual, leisurely, his planning careful and deliberate. For a while, he and Spiegel considered a film based on the life of Gandhi, but after thinking over some of the difficulties, political and logistic, they might encounter, they put this project temporarily aside. (It has subsequently been carried out in another Academy Award–winning epic directed by Sir Richard Attenborough, a minor player in *In Which We Serve.*) They then turned to the legendary T. E. Lawrence—"Lawrence of Arabia"—whose memoir, *The Seven Pillars of Wisdom,* had recently become available. (The rights had long been held by Alexander Korda, and at various times throughout the 1930s, 1940s, and 1950s, Robert Donat, Leslie Howard, Laurence Olivier, Dirk Bogarde, and Alec Guinness had been set to star in one or another Lawrence film.) Michael Wilson, who had worked (uncredited) on *The Bridge on the River Kwai,* wrote an initial treatment based on *Seven Pillars.* Not entirely satisfied with the results, Spiegel and Lean asked British playwright Robert Bolt, the author of *A Man for All Seasons,* to write the script. Finding the right actor to portray Lawrence was more of a problem. Lean would have liked Marlon Brando but was unable to get him. After offering the role to Albert Finney, who turned it down, Lean decided on Peter O'Toole, then virtually unknown to film audiences, whom he surrounded with a supporting cast of seasoned professionals.

Lean's *Lawrence of Arabia* exemplifies, extends, revises, mystifies, distorts, elucidates, revivifies one of the most compelling heroic myths of the twentieth century. From the moment his exploits became known, the character and actions of T. E. Lawrence captured the imagination of writers and readers everywhere. The Lawrence legend has not been an exclusively literary creation, however. Indeed, it is not the printed word that

Peter O'Toole as T. E. Lawrence.

first gave form to the portrait of Lawrence that has come down to us. Although many would credit Lowell Thomas's 1926 book *With Lawrence in Arabia* with the primary responsibility for popularizing and glorifying Lawrence's adventures, it was Thomas's earlier (1919–20) film/lecture program "With Allenby in Palestine and Lawrence in Arabia" that once and for all transformed a fairly obscure young Englishman into a full-fledged romantic hero. Thomas's media spectacle of the Arabian campaign, perhaps the most successful "show" of its kind in history, began with a live prologue evoking a moonlit evening on the Nile, the sets and costumes (from the opera *Joseph*) courtesy of Sir Thomas Beecham. But it was the film shot by Thomas's cameraman Harry Chase that truly captivated audiences. Speaking more or less ex tempore while the film was running, and accompanied by the Royal Welsh Guards Band, Thomas wove an Arabian Nights spell. "Mr. Lowell Thomas," Lawrence wrote at the time, "made me a kind of matinee idol."[1] It is precisely as a matinee idol that Lawrence returns to the screen and achieves an apotheosis of sorts in *Lawrence of Arabia*.

The myth of T. E. Lawrence was founded on paradox. Virtually from the moment he became a public figure, Lawrence inspired contradictory responses from those who came under his spell. Hostility and mistrust exist side by side with an admiration frequently verging on hero-worship. His stock has risen and fallen at regular intervals. Both as a private individual and as a public figure, Lawrence's reputation suffered a particularly severe blow with the publication, in 1953, of Richard Aldington's *T. E. Lawrence: a Biographical Inquiry*. This curiously shrill exercise in debunking calls into question virtually every claim Lawrence has on our interest and sympathy. But even if we refuse to give credence to Aldington's hatchet job, a dispassionate look at the record reveals a man whose actions and indeed whose very being can only be apprehended through a haze of ambiguity and paradox. Which may explain why, quite apart from our current preoccupation with the notion of imperialism and with the politics of the Middle East, he continues to intrigue and fascinate us.

Three particularly absorbing contradictions find roughly equivalent expression in the film. These might be schematized as follows:

1. *The Weakness/Strength Paradox*. The slight, short, pale, ascetic, aesthetic T. E. Lawrence, an Oxonian with a schoolgirl giggle, connoisseur of fine printed books, collector of brass rubbings, perhaps homosexual, perhaps asexual, almost certainly masochistic, versus the courageous, dashing, magnetic Oriental Lawrence, Prince of Mecca, uncrowned King of Arabia, bravely enduring torture, thirst, hunger and hundreds of other miseries and discomforts in a noble cause. Wrote W. H. Auden (employing categories borrowed from Christopher Isherwood): "To me Lawrence's life is an allegory of the transformation of the Truly Weak Man into the Truly Strong Man."[2]

2. *The Good/Bad Imperialist Paradox.* The Lawrence who wants to lead an oppressed people from bondage to freedom, who loves the East, the desert nights, the strength and courage of his Bedouin comrades, who can love an Arab boy with passion and kindness, who fights for Prince Feisal at Versailles; and the Lawrence who wants to make Arabia the first "brown" dominion, who hides knowledge of the infamous Sykes-Picot agreement from his Arab friends, who sells out Feisal at the Peace Conference, who finds himself personally soiled by contact with the Arabs, who can write that "for an Englishman to put himself at the disposal of a red race is to sell himself to a brute, like Swift's Houhynyms."

3. *The Paradox of Self-Promotion/Self-Abnegation.* On the one hand, the posturing Lawrence, posing for Lowell Thomas's photographer dressed in flamboyant white robes, collaborating on biographies with Thomas, with Robert Graves, with Basil Lidell-Hart, constructing a massive literary edifice, *The Seven Pillars of Wisdom,* on the foundation of his heroic exploits; on the other hand, the Lawrence who hides out in a London attic, who discourages biographers, who continually delays publication of his memoirs, who enters the RAF and the Tank Corps as a private, constantly changing his name: Ross, Shaw, Chapman, "T. E. Lawrence."

It is on the contradictions themselves, much more than on any specific account of Lawrence's life, that David Lean and Robert Bolt constructed their version of Lawrence. In doing so, they limited their narrative to selected key events from the Arab campaign. We see nothing of Lawrence before or after the war outside of the opening sequence dramatizing his death. The remainder of the film—a flashback of sorts—focuses on four events in particular: the conquest of Akaba, Lawrence's capture and torture in Deraa, the massacre at Tafas, and the fall of Damascus. Two military victories—the first relatively minor strategically but almost unambiguously glorious, the second major but fraught with ironies—frame two personal crises central to Lawrence's psychic life. Interspersed throughout are various confrontations, journeys, and military skirmishes, all of which enrich and complicate the meaning of the film's larger structural units.

Lawrence of Arabia does not attempt to present or to explain the "real" T. E. Lawrence (whoever he was); it is a fiction like all films, even those that aspire to documentary truth. The person who was T. E. Lawrence does not and could not exist in the film. As soon as he appears on the screen, the Lean/Bolt/Peter O'Toole Lawrence takes on a life independent of historical fact. All the same, the film from time to time draws upon extracinematic Lawrences (Lowell Thomas's Lawrence, Richard Aldington's Lawrence, and, of course, Lawrence's Lawrence). At such moments, we the audience are able to compare other texts to the filmic text, insofar as those texts are available to us. Nevertheless, the film presents its own, self-contained world. *Lawrence of Arabia* is, among other things, an essay on the paradox of heroism, on the inevitable, unfathomable fissures that separate impulse from act, history from myth, the self from the image of the self. Lean and his collaborators make no attempt to resolve the paradoxes I have outlined above; rather, they interknit and transform them in such a way as to enrich, in filmic terms, the texture of the Lawrence myth.

The first paradox—Weak Man/Strong Man—finds expression in *Lawrence of Arabia* primarily in terms of Lawrence's psychosexuality: as is true of the various written accounts of the historical Lawrence, suggestions of homosexuality, masochism, and sadism inform the film's text. Here, ambiguities are especially pronounced: censorship, in 1962, maintained its strong grip on the commercial cinema. Thus, homoeroticism is simultaneously repressed and exhibited by the text. For many viewers, this coyness probably resolves itself into an assertion of Lawrence's homosexuality. Since sexual "deviancy" has nearly always been treated obliquely and ambiguously in the mainstream cinema, obliqueness and ambiguity themselves signify the presence of what is absent. When the forbidden can only be hinted at, only a hint is necessary. The homosexual subtext serves primarily as metaphor, however, and is to some extent displaced by the foregrounding of sadomasochism as a thematic issue. In any case, insofar as Lawrence's psychosexual anxieties might, from a normative point of view, be considered a weakness, it is part of the film's project to transform that weakness into a strength. Lean and Bolt create a Lawrence who achieves heroism, however qualified that heroism might be, precisely because, in Christopher Isherwood's phrase, he "suffered, in his own person, the neurotic ills of an entire generation."[3]

Whether or not we finally see the film's Lawrence as homosexual is thus of secondary importance; of more interest is the film's equation of a conventionally coded set of mannerisms with effeminacy and, hence, weakness. This equation is stated at the outset; indeed, it is built into Peter O'Toole's performance as Lawrence. His manner and bearing, his gestures and body language, while suggesting a combination of diffidence and quirky individuality, also signify a stereotypical "gayness": O'Toole, particularly in the early scenes, projects a—for the lack of a better word—"fey" image, looking uncomfortably rumpled and decidedly unsoldierly in uniform. None of this is lost on General Murray (Donald Wolfit), the commanding officer whose contempt for Lawrence ("You're the kind of creature I can't stand") seems in excess of any motivation explicitly provided by the discourse. After agreeing to let Lawrence set off on an arduous and dangerous journey to find Prince Feisal, Murray remarks, "Who knows—might even make a man of him." The comment, in retrospect, is deeply ironic. On the one hand, becoming a "man" in the sense of passing from boyhood to manhood, is precisely what stirring adventure stories like *Lawrence of Arabia* are supposed to be about. Specifically, the film shows how an epicene young Englishman proves himself as courageous, resourceful, and strong as any hardened Arab chieftain. At the same time,

Top: Attack on a train in Lawrence of Arabia. *Bottom: Donald Wolfit (seated), Claude Rains, and Peter O'Toole in* Lawrence of Arabia.

Donald Wolfit's underscoring of the phrase "might even make a man of him" suggests something else: the distaste of the man of action, sexually self-confident, unthinkingly heterosexual, for the (seemingly) sexually neuter, perhaps homosexual, aesthete. Do Lawrence's subsequent experiences make a man of him? In Murray's terms, they do. Lawrence becomes a great military hero. But he becomes a "man" in another sense Murray could not have intended, for what Lawrence discovers at the end of his Arab adventures is his own humanity, his "manhood" as a member of the human race. Along the way, he is tempted by "godhood," a temptation that transcends "manhood" entirely and ends by making a mockery of Murray's straightforward wish.

The temptation of godhood as a theme in *Lawrence of Arabia* hardly needs elucidating, so self-consciously have Lean and Bolt woven it into their text. This theme manifests itself in Lawrence's increasing isolation, in his donning of spotless white robes that give him visual predominance over the particolored Arabs, in the worshipful attitudes of his followers, and, most notably, in his abrogating to himself the right to execute a man ostensibly because, as an Englishman, he stands above petty tribal rivalries and age-old blood feuds. By presenting Lawrence as a kind of god to the Arabs, the film seems to reenact one of the hoariest clichés found in Hollywood films set in "primitive" cultures and among "savage" tribes: the white Westerner who is mistaken for a deity by the dark, superstitious natives. Normally, however, this scenario involves a woman, the "White Jungle Queen" of Edward Field's poem. Which suggests an intriguing speculation. In a film where women are conspicuous by their absence, Lawrence—pale, effeminate, a blond and blue-eyed seraph—becomes a surrogate woman, a figurative white goddess. An ambiguous exchange of dialogue points nicely in this direction. Immediately after the fall of Akaba, Sherif Ali (played by the darkly handsome and self-consciously masculine Omar Sharif) brings Lawrence flowers, tossing them on the water at his feet. "Garlands for the conqueror, tributes for the prince, flowers for the man," Ali says. "I'm none of these things, Ali," Lawrence responds. If Lawrence is not conqueror, prince, or man, we might reasonably ask, what is he? Without pushing an admittedly shaky speculation any further, we can note that Lawrence constantly seduces the various Arabs to his view of things, making them love him as well as follow him. "You trouble me like women," Auda says to Lawrence and Ali in the course of one of the most important of these "seductions." However we read the line, Lawrence's manipulative tactics with the Arabs are here clearly exposed as "feminine" wiles. A supposed weakness—Lawrence's effeminacy—is thus transformed into a strength.

Textually allied to Lawrence's effeminacy is his masochism. Moments after the film introduces us to the young Lawrence, an army lieutenant stationed in Cairo, we see him demonstrating his physical self-control by slowly snuffing out a burning match with his fingers. Right off, Lawrence's status as "hero" is complicated and qualified. It is notable that Lawrence performs this trick in front of puzzled but admiring "other rankers"; already, he is an exhibitionist, albeit on a small scale. When one of the soldiers tries to repeat Lawrence's performance, he quickly pulls his hand away from the match, complaining that "it hurts." "Of course it hurts," Lawrence replies. "What's the trick, then?" the soldier asks. "The trick," Lawrence responds, "is in not minding that it hurts." Soon afterwards, having received permission to go into Arabia, Lawrence lights another match, but this time he blows it out in the normal way. By cutting from an enormous close-up of the match to a shot of the burning desert, Lean implies that Lawrence's penetration of Arabia, whatever else may motivate him, functions as a displacement of his masochism, a painful/pleasurable testing of the self. By stages, both the pain and the pleasure increase to an extent Lawrence could not have foreseen. When pain and pleasure, even at their most intense, can no longer be distinguished from each other, Lawrence has reached the breaking point: beyond it lies madness.

The breaking point comes at Deraa, but even before Deraa, his experiences force Lawrence to question his own actions and motives. He knows that war is progressively corrupting him, that he has failed to gauge how much his own dreams and plans involve bloodshed. Most frightening of all, as he confesses to General Allenby (Jack Hawkins), he has come to enjoy the bloodshed. Faced with such self-knowledge, he can only ask Allenby to relieve him from further duty with the Arabs. But Allenby cannot let him go, for Lawrence has become a hero, and his heroism is too useful a weapon to cast aside. At this point, there is a break in the filmic text, a break of such magnitude that it must be covered by an intermission. The intense young hero of the film's first half turns into the cynical and vainglorious poseur of the second half while the audience buys popcorn in the lobby. With a boldness remarkable in the commercial cinema, Lean simply omits what would appear to be a crucial transition and thus leaves the audience to its own devices.

When, after the intermission, the film resumes, the first figure we see is Bentley (Arthur Kennedy), the cynical newspaperman very loosely modeled on Lowell Thomas (who was never cynical, at least in public, about Lawrence). Bentley's appearance underlines the shift in focus between the film's two major parts. Lawrence is by now a public figure, a "hero" created by Bentley; ironically, his fame seems to have diminished his responsibilities. Now more of a sideshow than anything else, he and his guerrilla bands derail and loot Turkish trains. A hero in the eyes of the Arabs, he appears vain and childish in ours. The film, at this point, credits Lawrence's debunkers. When Lawrence says of the Turks, "They can only kill me with a golden bullet," his words seem not nearly as ironic as he would like them to be. Soon afterwards, in his "mercy killing" of an adoring Arab servant, Lawrence finds himself once again responsible for the death of someone close to him (he earlier executed Gassim, the man he brought out of the Nefud desert, and he lost his other servant boy, Daoud, in quicksand). Being a god means sacrificing merely human bonds. Shortly after this, through his experience in Deraa, Lawrence finally comes face to face with his simple mortality, his need for a "ration of common humanity."

The film's presentation of the Deraa episode may fairly be criticized as irritatingly oblique. Lawrence, disguised as a poor Arab, enters the Turkish stronghold at Deraa on a reconnaissance mission. Picked up by Turkish soldiers (after making himself quite conspicuous), he is brought before the local Bey (José Ferrer), who appears to be more than professionally interested in discovering an Arab with fair skin and blue eyes. In resisting the Bey's clearly sexual advances, Lawrence knees him sharply in the groin. The Bey's guards, degenerate-looking specimens who take obvious sadistic pleasure in their task, flog Lawrence mercilessly and then throw him out into the night. Lawrence, in *The Seven Pillars of Wisdom,* describes his experience with some hesitation and circumlocution, but nevertheless with an overall frankness that caused him considerable pain. As he vividly tells it, the guards not only beat him but also played "unspeakably" with him; when the beating was nearly over, Lawrence felt "a delicious warmth, probably sexual," swelling through him. After one final slash of the whip into his groin, he tells us, "my eyes went black: while within me the core of life seemed to heave slowly up through the rending nerves, expelled from its body by this last indescribable pang." Nothing in his account, however, altogether explains his summary judgment of his experience. "In Deraa that night," he writes, "the citadel of my integrity had been irrevocably lost."[4]

I cite Lawrence's account, the only one we have of the Deraa experience, not so much to counteract as to rationalize the film's obliqueness. Censorship aside, both Lawrence's own mysteriousness and the film's constant refusal to explain away complex experiences justify an indirect approach. Whatever else Deraa may mean, it signifies in the film that moment when Lawrence recognizes the fundamental frailty of his flesh as well as his frightening ability to transcend that frailty. The Truly Weak Man and the Truly Strong Man come acutely together for a moment, and the Lawrence who emerges from the experience is a different Lawrence from the one who walked boldly into Deraa. That the Truly Strong Man turns briefly to sadism can then be seen as a necessary prelude to self-awareness, to a final revulsion from and abdication of his godlike heroism: having entered into the heart of darkness, Lawrence discovers a horrible image of himself.

The Conradian allusion may aptly preface a look at Lawrence's relationship with the Arabs, or what I have termed the Paradox of the Good/Bad Imperialist. We need to read this aspect of the film with particular care, since Lean and Bolt are not always as conscious of the paradox as we might like. The truly "bad" imperialists are certainly easy enough to identify. The suave, cynical Dryden (Claude Rains) and the seemingly apolitical Allenby ("I'm just a soldier, thank God") epitomize the political/military complex we know as imperialism. Lawrence, as we would expect, is relatively enlightened. When he invades the Officers Club in Cairo—clearly a hotbed of racism—dressed as an Arab and accompanied by his Arab servant, we are made to feel, along with Lawrence, superior to the obvious imperialists. Actually, Lawrence merely asserts his ego in this scene; politics has been subsumed by private virtues, and private virtues, as we all know, all too often become public vices. Here and elsewhere, the film suppresses the central issue of imperialism: that it is the "good" imperialists, idealists like Lawrence, who prepare the way for the bad ones. "The English," Prince Feisal tells Lawrence, "have a great hunger for desolate places." Lawrence clearly shares that hunger, and though his appetite may be personal rather than national, born of admiration rather than ambition, it is equally imperial to the hunger of a Dryden or an Allenby.

Idealist or no, Lawrence, like all imperialists, wishes to dominate, to impose *his* will, *his* vision, *his* understanding of what is good for *them* on the Arabs whose life he shares and whose aspirations he claims to value. The film in fact presents the Arab world with some ambivalence, as the casting strategies alone might lead one to expect. Some of the actors (notably the Egyptian Omar Sharif) are Orientals; Feisal, however, is portrayed by Alec Guinness, very much an Englishman, and Auda Abu Tayi by the Mexican-American actor Anthony Quinn. These three characters embody the range of stereotypes Western culture holds of Arabs. Feisal is sage, calm, softspoken, prophetlike; Auda is childish, excitable, vain, avaricious—all emotionalism and sensuality; Ali incorporates elements of both, while additionally contributing attractive exoticism and "Oriental" glamour. Insofar as *Lawrence of Arabia* presents the Arabs as greedy, irascible, quarrelsome, "simple," earthy, and so forth, it fails to escape the preconceptions of much of its audience; instead, it enters into the dilemma of its protagonist. Lawrence attempts to identify with the Arabs by becoming one. Having no identity of his own (he is, as he explains to Ali, a bastard), he is willingly adopted—literally—by his Arab friends. But identities cannot be acquired so easily; he is not, after all, an Arab, and the more he tries to be one, the more emphatic his alienation becomes. We see this immediately after the fall of Akaba when, alone, Lawrence rides his camel by the seashore, cut off from human contact, incapable of relishing a victory that is not really his. But taking on an Arab identity does help Lawrence further the imperial project. He wins the Arabs over primarily by demonstrating that he is as good as they are; he is then perceived—in the film, at least—as better. For Lawrence seemingly conquers fate; for him, "nothing is written." He thus combines the virtues and strengths of the Arabs with a freedom from their strict ethical and social codes. His power, which gives him the upper hand, grows from these attributes.

In stages, as I have already noted, Lawrence becomes like a god, neither English nor Arab, deciding who shall live and who shall die, executing justice free of emotional involvement, responsible to no one but himself. So, in order to prevent his followers from disintegrating on the eve of the battle for Akaba, he cold-bloodedly executes a man he had earlier rescued from certain death. The ambiguities of his role are perfectly symbolized by this act: seemingly dealing even-handed justice, he actually serves the imperial will. In the end, the idea that nothing is written, that man makes his own fate, becomes Lawrence's greatest delusion, for he forgets, as we are seldom allowed to, the nature of the powers that circumscribe his actions. Thus self-deceived, Lawrence becomes himself a victim of imperialism, an ideology that frequently prefers to give the illusion of independence while keeping a tight hold on the reins of power.

Simultaneously an imperialist and the victim of imperialism, Lawrence must fail equally in his attempt to transcend political realities and personal limitations. The ambiguities in Lawrence's character, his inability to come to terms with his own actions, his progressive alienation from everything around him, signify an overwhelming guilt that can be read as the projection of the collective disease we call imperialism. Lawrence, like Robert Bolt's Sir Thomas More in *A Man for All Seasons*, finds himself caught between the demands of the world and the promptings of his conscience; unlike More, however, Lawrence cannot bring the conflict into absolute clarity. And so, also unlike More, he cannot see his way out of the dilemma. A hero who has outlived the age of heroes, Lawrence finds no decisive victory at the end of his quest. The capture of Damascus is a bitter anticlimax, the Arabs remain as divided as ever, British masters are substituted for Turkish ones, and even Prince Feisal turns to cynicism. "Colonel Lawrence," he tells Allenby, "is a sword with two edges: we are equally glad to be rid of him, are we not?"

But if Lawrence is quintessentially modern in his heroism, it is not because he fails in his quest—other heroes have failed before him—but because of the intensely self-conscious way he acts out his heroic role. Lawrence simultaneously performs as a hero and watches himself performing. And we, of course, watch him performing as well. The Paradox of Self-Promotion/Self-Abnegation is transformed into the tension between role and identity. It is here that David Lean most brilliantly employs film in such a way that its formal properties reflect the thematics of the fable. A theatrical medium, film perfectly captures the undeniably exhibitionist constituents of Lawrence's personality. Lean and Bolt eagerly borrow upon and expand details of fact and myth that stress Lawrence's self-consciousness, his bent for playacting, his awareness of the value of gesture and pose. (In *Seven Pillars*, Lawrence writes of his "detached self always eyeing the performance from the wings in criticism."[5]) Peter O'Toole calls attention throughout to Lawrence as performer, which inevitably makes us aware of his own "performance" as Lawrence. Indeed, one of the film's special pleasures lies in the playfulness O'Toole brings to his characterization, a playfulness that suggests his own enjoyment at play-acting on such a grand scale—and in his first major film at that! Performance thus becomes an issue both outside of as well as within the diegesis. By casting the virtually unknown O'Toole as Lawrence, Lean complicates the categories of actor, role, and identity. Since, in the cinema, character and actor cannot easily be distinguished, O'Toole, with no "star" persona to interfere, at once embodies and individualizes Lawrence. And O'Toole is supported by well-known stars whose very presence insures immediate identification: Jack Hawkins, lending his solid, gruff Britishness to General Allenby; Alec Guinness, providing Feisal with dry wit and gentle intelligence; Anthony Quinn doing his turn as aging macho ethnic. Because these actors are not fundamentally mysterious, their characters are not mysterious. They thus serve to emphasize by contrast O'Toole's unknownness, an unknownness that then encompasses Lawrence himself. These casting strategies also contribute meaning to a subsidiary but related theme; Lawrence, the young upstart lieutenant, takes over the Arab revolt supported by the older and more experienced Allenby, Feisal, and Auda, just as O'Toole, the young upstart actor, takes over the film supported by seasoned actors like Hawkins, Guinness, and Quinn.

Self-dramatization, in one form or another, nearly always colors Lawrence's behavior. Even his most heroic moments are qualified by self-conscious gesture. The climactic event in the film's first movement—up to the fall of Akaba—shows us Lawrence courageously and with single-minded determination retracing his steps through the murderous Nefud desert to rescue a lost Arab comrade. Lean uses all of the tools at his disposal—photography, composition, editing, music—to construct one of the film's best-remembered sequences. In a rhythmic series of alternating shots we see the Arab, Gassim, wandering aimlessly under an ever-intensifying sun, Lawrence determinedly riding toward him, the servant-boy anxiously waiting at the desert's edge, and finally a culminating image of Lawrence, baked and parched, his face seemingly sandblasted to a gray mask, galloping out of the desert on his camel, the half-dead Gassim holding on to him quite literally for dear life. Interestingly, Lawrence's account of this episode in *Seven Pillars of Wisdom* is, as is usual with him, self-deprecatingly unheroic; in the film, his doubts, qualifications, and hesitations are suppressed. Nevertheless, the whole sequence is so formal in its structure, so manipulative and yet meticulous in its construction, as to simultaneously draw us in and keep us at a distance. We are made uncomfortably aware that Lawrence acts as much to demonstrate his courage and heroic temper—to the Arabs and to himself—as he does to save the life of a fellow human being.

Very soon after this exploit, Lawrence, at the instigation of Ali, assumes Arab dress, a costume (in every sense of the word) of spotless white. Emblematically, at least, Lawrence is now an Arab. At the same time, he looks like no other Arab in the film; rather than taking on the identity of his comrades, he assumes a visually unique role. Lean stresses the theatrical nature of the transformation by having Lawrence ride off by himself as soon as he has put on his new costume. Finding an isolated spot, Lawrence dismounts and begins to prance and posture to his own shadow, allowing the flowing robes to balloon behind him in the breeze. He is a little boy dressing up, acting out Arabian Nights heroics. Here, in particular, we sense the actor behind the role. Lawrence and O'Toole seem to be both reveling in and in awe of the part they are playing, uncertain of what to do next but at the same time aware that from now on there is no turning back: destiny calls. The moment is privileged: Lawrence will never again seem at once so winning and so vulnerable.

If Lawrence is an actor, Arabia is his stage. The metaphor, as Edward Said more than once suggests in *Orientalism,* implicitly informs much of the Western literature that concerns itself with Arabia. "The Orient is the stage on which the whole East is confined. . . ," Said writes, "a theatrical stage whose audience, manager, and actors are *for* Europe, and only for Europe."[6] Lean fills *Lawrence of Arabia* with flamboyantly theatrical shots of Middle Eastern topography, but those critics who fault the director for indulging in breathtaking vistas for their own sake miss the point entirely. Just as, in earlier films, he painstakingly used plaster and lath as a method of re-creating a subjective reality (Dickens's London in *Oliver Twist*, for example) so here he takes great pains to formalize the real world until it begins to resemble an impossibly elaborate studio set. Lean's remarkable pans and tracks of the desert sands, his complicated zooms, his compositions revealing the mysterious mirages of the desert, his dramatic visual surprises—as when a ship looms over the edge of a sand dune—are all directed toward establishing Arabia Deserta as a series of fabulous backdrops for Lawrence's exploits.

But the more Lawrence penetrates the landscape, the more he seems to absorb it into himself: Arabia is a theater in Lawrence's mind. "The passage of the mythological hero," Joseph Campbell reminds us, "may be overground, incidentally; fundamentally it is inward—into depths where obscure resistances are overcome, and long lost, forgotten powers are revivified."[7] Lean's epic style depicts Arabia as both a magnificent stage set and a metaphysical landscape, his elegantly tracking camera capturing the grandeur and barrenness of the desert, his slow dissolves and subliminal editing suggesting the illogical continuity and dreamlike texture of the forbidding terrain. Initially dwarfed by the desert's vastness and buffeted by its inexorable brutality, Lawrence learns to come to terms with it, to become at once part of it and apart from it. He inhabits this world, as he does everything, self-consciously: grandiloquent of gesture, ostentatious, vainglorious, he plays his part as well as he can for a man who does not know what his part really is.

Role-playing on this scale can lead to the borders of schizophrenia. Twice in the film, Lawrence looks at his own reflection in the blade of his knife. In the first instance, he is still relatively innocent. He has just put on his white robes for the first time, and he studies the image reflected back to him in puzzled admiration, not quite believing that he has been able so thoroughly and drastically to change his identity. The second time, much later in the film, the context is very different. Lawrence, after giving the order to take no prisoners, participates in the massacre at Tafas. The white robes are now soiled with blood, and the face Lawrence submits to reflective scrutiny seems to be that of a madman. Neither man nor role is recognizably what they were before, and Lawrence can now only retreat from heroism, put aside his Arab dress, and return to England and the absurd, perhaps not entirely accidental death with which the film began.

The paradoxes I have been discussing do not, in Lean's film, resolve themselves into a solution to the enigma of Lawrence's character. *Lawrence of Arabia* ends, as it began, a deeply ambiguous film; indeed, it ends and begins simultaneously. Lawrence enters the film in order to die. As his motorcycle speeds along a country road, his intense face is illuminated by areas of light and shadow in alternation, an effect that becomes more and more bizarre as his velocity increases. Swerving to avoid hitting someone on the road, he loses control of his machine and, thrown offscreen, quite literally disappears. Here, in the first moments of the film, we have the essential Lawrence: brave but foolhardy; a thrillseeker who seems to invite disaster; manic intensity; a self-sacrificial bravado; a fatal gesture; the superhuman will in conflict with human possibilities; the hero as scapegoat.

Such a beginning to what most viewers would rightly consider a rousing adventure story should warn us to expect a film that constantly questions itself, not only in terms of plot, character, and theme but also as a particular kind of discourse, as a method of presentation. Lowell Thomas's film created a hero; Lean's film, at least in part, is about the power of the cinema to create a hero. Though Lawrence's motives may be beyond recovery, his image speaks eloquently to our hopes and needs. Time and again, Lean's camera closes in on Lawrence's face as if to penetrate its mystery, and each close-up leaves us with a deeper enigma than before. The image cannot be questioned; it is inviolate. But if he refuses to solve the puzzle of Lawrence's character, Lean brilliantly depicts Lawrence's world. He thus transcends and at the same time pays homage to film as spectacle. Allusive, open, self-conscious, mystifying, unfinished, complex, *Lawrence of Arabia* remains one of the richest and most satisfying of modern epics.

8

Doctor Zhivago (1965) and *Ryan's Daughter* (1970)

LEAN HAD NOW reached the peak of his critical and commercial success. He would make only two more films, neither of which achieved the balance of popular appeal and formal complexity characteristic of *Lawrence of Arabia*. In terms of box-office receipts, *Doctor Zhivago* was an even greater success than its predecessor, grossing some $30 million at a time when admission prices were still relatively low. The critics, however, were not nearly as charmed as was the public, and even the Motion Picture Academy began to cool in its ardor, awarding the film only five Oscars, none of which was in the top five categories. Having made three of the most popular films of all time, Lean was no longer taken seriously by the critical establishment. *Ryan's Daughter*, released after a five-year silence, only confirmed the judgment of Lean's most hostile critics. The reviews were devastating and the public was not much interested, either: for the first time in years, a Lean film lost money. Its failure was for Lean a bitter disappointment. Although new projects, including *Gandhi*, *A Tale of Two Cities*, and *Captain Bligh and Mr. Christian*, would be announced from time to time, none of them has come to fruition. Lean seemingly retired from the screen.

Doctor Zhivago (1965)

The publication of Boris Pasternak's *Doctor Zhivago*, first in an unauthorized Italian translation in 1957 and subsequently in an English version in 1958, was greeted by the so-called free world with extraordinary enthusiasm. Edmund Wilson, dean of American journalist-critics, heralded Pasternak's banned-in-the-USSR novel as "one of the great events in man's literary and moral history,"[1] comparing Pasternak to Pushkin and Tolstoy. In October 1958, Pasternak was awarded the Nobel Prize for literature primarily on the basis of *Doctor Zhivago*. Today, some twenty-five years after the event, it may seem incomprehensible that this thin (for all of its five hundred pages) and uninspired imitation of a nineteenth-century Russian novel could have been greeted as a work of genius. The saga of a

Geraldine Chaplin and Omar Sharif in Dr. Zhivago.

doctor/poet who lives through the great social upheavals of war and revolution while balancing obligations to his family and a passion for his mistress, Pasternak's novel never really comes to life. His characters are crudely sketched; his plot meanders; his ideas are shallow and labored; his structure is haphazard and confusing. *Doctor Zhivago,* in short, is a very bad book. Only when we recall that the novel appeared at the height of the Cold War does its reception begin to make sense. The blurb on the New American Library paperback edition unwittingly suggests a cause-and-effect relationship by describing *Doctor Zhivago* as "the great novel that was suppressed in Russia . . . praised as a masterpiece throughout the free world." Such a confusion of aesthetics and politics—or rather the absorption of the former by the latter—perfectly symbolizes the mood of the American 1950s.

In adapting Pasternak's novel for the screen, Lean and scriptwriter Robert Bolt did not violate the spirit of a major literary work, as some reviewers thought. Instead, they lent spurious distinction to a highbrow potboiler. True, both men gave the impression, in public pronouncements, of holding the novel in high regard. It therefore comes as a pleasant surprise to discover how thoroughly their adaptation ignores it. Bolt, in his "Author's Note" prefacing the published screenplay of *Doctor Zhivago,* theorizes about the process of adaptation in general, listing four reasons for the necessary differences between a novel and a film: (1) "mere length" (a faithful adaptation of *Doctor Zhivago,* he surmises, would run for forty-five hours); (2) "the mechanical differences between a narrative and a dramatic form"; (3) the difficulty in dealing with the reflections of the novelist; (4) the need to maintain an unbroken progression from beginning to end that film form demands.[2] His points are valid enough as far as they go, but they hardly prepare us for what follows. The screenplay Bolt and Lean together fashioned ("We fought our way line by line and even sometimes shot by shot from one end of the screenplay to the other, many times over"[3]) retains the central characters (more or less altered), an outline of the plot, and some of Pasternak's major thematic concerns. The film's structure, many of the characterizations, most of the specific episodes, and virtually all of the dialogue are either original with the filmmakers or highly imaginative transformations of details from the novel.

Many of the film's most distinctive elements have no original in the novel: the flashback structure and Yevgref's narration; the balalaika and, in general, the association of Lara with Yuri's mother; Yuri and Lara's first encounter on the streetcar; Pasha's prewar revolutionary activities; the intertwining of the Komarovsky-Lara tryst with the street demonstration; Komarovsky's (semi-)rape of Lara; many of the details surrounding Yuri's postwar homecoming, including the partitioned house and the firewood-stealing episode; the boarded-up house at Yuriatin; the ice-castle. At the same time, of course, a good deal of the novel's texture, its attempt to create a detailed context for action and character, has been eliminated, with some resulting simplification. Motives that remain vague and unexplained in the novel frequently become explicit in the film, and the script telescopes historical events, often reducing fairly complex ideas to simple slogans. Nevertheless, the script improves on the novel in nearly every way, highlighting thematic issues, bringing form out of shapelessness, creating vivid characters from vague shadows, and eliminating much pseudophilosophical nonsense in the bargain. What virtues the film has are primarily the filmmakers' contribution; its failures, for the most part, are the novel's failures.

Interestingly, minor details from the novel, remembered by the adaptor and expressed visually, often take on a larger significance than they originally had. The candle in the window, discussed below, provides one instance of this. Lara working as a nurse in the makeshift army hospital provides another. Zhivago discovers her ironing with "two flat irons" that she "used alternately, putting them each in turn in the flue to keep them hot."[4] This virtually insignificant detail, realized precisely and visually foregrounded in the film, gives Lara a substance and seriousness, a nobility, even, that we must otherwise accept on faith. As in the novel, ironing also links Lara with Tonya. Watching his wife iron long after his hospital service, Pasternak's Zhivago writes in his journal: "It reminds me of something, but I can't think of what" (!).[5] The film is less heavy-handed than Pasternak; we simply see Zhivago looking at his wife ironing and we know, as he does, of what he is reminded.

At the same time, in any reasonably ambitious work of fiction some elements virtually defy transference to another medium. *Doctor Zhivago*, whatever its failings, is not a conventional novel; it aspires to the "poetic" and the mystical. Take, for instance, this passage, crucial to Pasternak's purpose:

> Ever since his childhood Yuri Andreievich had been fond of woods seen at evening against the setting sun. At such moments he felt as if he too were being pierced by shafts of light. It was as though the gift of the living spirit were streaming into his breast, piercing his being and coming out at his shoulders like a pair of wings. The archetype that is formed in every child for life and seems for ever after to be his inward face, his personality, awoke in him in its full primordial strength, and compelled nature, the forest, the afterglow, and everything else visible to be transfigured into a similarly primordial and all-embracing likeness of a girl. Closing his eyes, "Lara," he whispered and thought, addressing the whole of his life, all God's earth, all the sunlit space spread out before him.[6]

Any literal enactment of this paragraph would be ludicrous. Lean nevertheless attempts with the resources at his command to interweave Yuri

Dr. Zhivago: *The Moscow set.*

Zhivago's spiritual communion with nature and his association of nature with Lara. However, as I will show, Lean places this romantic mysticism in a specific context, creating a highly subjective narrative structure and a deliberately "artificial" filmic world to contain and qualify Yuri Zhivago's vision.

The artifice of David Lean's *Doctor Zhivago* informs nearly every frame and pervades such elements as plot, structure, setting, color, camera movement, editing, music, and dialogue. Both to emphasize the subjectivity of the narrative as well as to maintain the objectivity of the viewer, Lean employs distancing techniques that call attention to the fictive world of the film. Much of *Doctor Zhivago* takes place as in a dream, an effect stressed by its mode of telling: the story of Yuri Zhivago, Lara, Tonya, and Pasha unfolds in one sustained flashback narrated by Yuri's half-brother Yevgref, who could not have been present at most of the events he narrates. Yevgref, by his own admission, functions as an unreliable narrator ("I think I even told him that we would meet again in better times; but perhaps I didn't"). Voice-over narration has a built-in distancing effect, but Lean carries the convention one step further. When Yevgref visits Yuri and his family in Moscow, his voice-over narrative continues as he converses with Yuri: we hear what other characters say, but we do not hear Yevgref's part of the conversation at all. His retrospective account takes precedence over the "present" images. Here Lean deliberately calls into question our ability to reconcile past and present, truth and memory, objective and subjective. At the same time, his method calls attention to itself, momentarily suspending our involvement in the action and thereby forcing us to think about what we are experiencing. We are signaled to treat Zhivago's story to some extent as myth, the film's characters and events having been reconstructed by report, rumor, and finally filtered through a sympathetic imagination. And reinforcing the influence of narrator on narration, the "frame" sequences are photographed in muted, "realistic" tones in contrast to the heightened coloring of the body of the film.

Even the film's varied settings—Spain, Italy, Yugoslavia, Scandinavia, and Canada—though they serve to provide the film with attractive background and decor, with majestic scenery and varied climates, have the further, paradoxical effect of giving the impression that the film takes place nowhere in particular. So careful was Lean in choosing locations that the film has a unified "studio" look. Locale has been internationalized to the point of being universalized. In tone with the large and impressive sets of Moscow built on the outskirts of Madrid, the whole film exhibits a storybook prettiness. *Doctor Zhivago* could just as well have been filmed entirely on a sound stage. In a sense, it has been: Lean has simply transformed the world into a movie studio. Lean, partly through the obvious artifice of his style, creates in *Doctor Zhivago* at once a romantic film and a critique of romanticism. The film's romanticism is self-conscious, its excesses are calculated, its surface beauty too good to be true. As *Lawrence of Arabia* deals with heroic illusion, *Doctor Zhivago*, like so many of Lean's films, is about romantic illusion.

Illusion is closely associated with vision, with what we see (literally as well as figuratively) and how we see it. In *Doctor Zhivago*, vision becomes a central theme. A complex of shots featuring windows and other transparent, translucent, and semiopaque surfaces structure the film. Some examples: the young girl (Zhivago's putative daughter) first appears behind a wire-meshed glass pane; Yuri, as a child, watches a storm through a frosted window; Lara sees the wounded Pasha appear behind semiopaque glass, initially mistaking him for Komarovsky; Yuri first sees Lara through a glass partition, which, like a theatrical scrim, becomes illuminated from the back and made transparent; Tonya welcomes the returning Zhivago from a balcony window; in the cattle car, Yuri searches for sky and light through a small windowlike opening; Pasha/Strelnikov watches Zhivago depart through the (bullet-proof?) window of his armored railroad car; Lara looks out of her cottage window and sees the ominous figure of Komarovsky; Yuri breaks a frosted pane to watch Lara's departure; from a trolley-car window, Yuri sees Lara for the last time. This recurrent motif implies, most obviously, an inside/outside dichotomy. Inside signifies warmth, comfort, safety, a settled life; outside signifies cold, discomfort, danger, challenge. Lean's camera frequently takes the viewpoint of characters inside looking out or outside looking in. Pasha, following Lara, watches her enter the Sventytski house and then looks up at a bright window just as the lights go out and the image changes to the newly lit Christmas tree within. An "outsider," Pasha cannot experience the warm domesticity that window represents. In contrast, Yuri, cooped up with his family in their snowbound cottage, looks longingly for spring—and, one knows, for Lara—through a frosted window; soon, the window is covered with frozen snowflakes that melt as the sun passes over them. Lean lap-dissolves to a field of gladioli, and Yuri's wish for spring and for Lara is realized. The yearning for something other than what one has, for a different life, finds expression through these "window shots."

Windows also imply voyeurism. As has often been noted, film is a voyeuristic medium; windows merely emphasize something already implicit (see almost any Hitchcock film, but especially *Rear Window* [1954]). When Lara's mother attempts suicide, Lean films Kamarovsky's frantic response from outside the house, his camera restlessly moving from window to window to keep up with Kamarovsky's panicky actions. The effect is twofold: we are made uncomfortably aware that we are prying into a very private and sordid event at the same time that we share Lean's detach-

Omar Sharif and Julie Christie in Dr. Zhivago.

ment from it. Later in the same sequence, Yuri wanders through the dressmaker's shop and comes to a glass partition (the "scrim" I referred to earlier) through which a woman's hand is dimly visible. A door opens, a light illuminates the other side of the glass, and we, like Yuri, realize that we are looking into Lara's bedroom, "spying," in spite of ourselves, as Kamarovsky comes to tell Lara her mother will live. (Lean, only a realist when it suits his purpose, plays fast and loose with the internal geography of the house here, it being highly unlikely that Lara's bedroom would be separated from the working area by a sheet of glass; the effect, however, is more than worth the cheating.)

In their use of windows, Lean and Bolt have in fact picked up on hints from the novel. The film's most effective use of this motif is also one of the most direct borrowings from Pasternak. In the novel, Lara attempts (and fails; she does not actually confess until the wedding night) to tell Pasha of her affair with Komarovsky. As they talk, Pasha lights a candle and puts it by the window. "A soft light filled the room," Pasternak writes. "In the sheet of ice covering the windowpane a black eyelet began to form at the level of the flame."[7] Moments later, Yuri and Tonya happen to pass by and Yuri notices "that a candle had melted a patch in the icy crust on one of the windows. The light seemed to look into the street almost consciously, as if it were watching the passing carriages and waiting for someone."[8] Lean and Bolt pick up on this image and use it as an occasion for another "discreet" window sequence. The first shot is from outside Pasha's frosted window, loud Christmas bells ringing on the soundtrack. We watch but cannot hear the at first indefinite figures of Pasha reading Lara's letter and Lara confessing all to Pasha. The candle slowly burns an increasingly larger hole in the icy film covering the window, its translucent surface becoming gradually transparent. The camera moves closer and closer to the window, eventually focusing on Lara's face. Lean then cuts to a reverse shot of the candle with the window behind it. The camera travels toward the window and cranes up to reveal a sleigh passing on the street below. Now we are with the sleigh as Yuri looks up at the window. Tonya, thinking back to the Christmas party, where she has seen Lara, says, "Yuri, where have you seen that girl before?" and Lean then follows the conversation in the sleigh. In an almost entirely visual manner (and, of course, with some help from Pasternak), Lean has brought the film's four main characters together at a key moment of crumbling illusions and lost innocence (the following sequence begins with the outbreak of World War I). The candle burning away the covering veil of ice also burns away the simple, idealistic world of an entire generation.

Complementing the window motif and supporting the dialectical themes of inside/outside, public/private, reality/illusion are various images of transparence, translucence, and semiopacity. A veil, for example, partially covers and softens the face of Yuri's mother as she is lowered into her grave. Later, in a moment charged with sexuality, Komarovsky places a veil over the lower part of Lara's face and then slowly removes it, a symbolic dressing and undressing which in a complex way alludes to Yuri's mother. One particularly striking translucent surface is the sheet of ice that covers a cattle-door and must be broken through to allow fresh air inside. When Yuri mistakenly believes he sees, in the distance, the family from which he has been long separated, the snowy, misty, windblown landscape creates a semitransparent barrier that suggests his failure in moral vision, his past inability to see his duty clearly.

Inside and outside, warmth and cold, fire and ice, illusion and reality, are all brought together visually when Yuri and Lara briefly inhabit the summer cottage at Yuriatin. Abandoned for years to the elements, the house has become an ice castle, a frozen world preserving the past as in aspic. Yuri and Lara enter it through a nearly opaque glass door that leads them through a room where the walls and furnishings are covered with snow, to a somewhat clearer glass door and finally to a room free of snow and ice. In this house, the interior has become the exterior; there is no inside or outside. It is here that Yuri writes his poetry, here that Lara and Yuri enjoy a respite from external demands. But, as the howling wolves outside warn, theirs is a brief, precarious idyll. Komarovsky reappears and the world reasserts its demands. Illusion, once again, gives way to reality.

Unlike Boris Pasternak's novel, which celebrates "Life" in a simple-minded, self-indulgent way, Lean's *Doctor Zhivago* permits a genuine dialectic among large and small oppositions and contrasts, in part through social (public/private), seasonal (summer/winter), and elemental (fire/ice) juxtapositions, but primarily through pairings of characters (Lara/Tonya; Komarovsky/Strelnikov; Zhivago/Strelnikov; Zhivago/Komarovsky). *Doctor Zhivago*'s plot does not rest on a triangle; rather, it is a complex pattern of parallel and intersecting lines. Pasternak's novel, of course, provides the source for much of this, but Lean and Bolt maintain—more scrupulously and more consistently than Pasternak—the tensions between conflicting impulses and ideas. This explains why, in spite of all the romantic coloring Zhivago's imagination lavishes on her, Lara does not emerge as an unequivocal object of an *amour fou.* The film's style (which includes such matters as casting choices) assures that the audience's sympathies will be as much with Zhivago's wife as with his mistress. Tonya, as portrayed by Geraldine Chaplin, genuinely grows in the course of the film. Initially little more than a pretty china doll, all dressed up in pinks and furs, her delicate features and naive enthusiasms suggesting the appealing asexuality of a child, she develops into a strong, self-reliant woman, more than worthy of Yuri's love and admiration. By contrast, Lara, in spite of Julie Christie's undeniable sensuality, has less substance than Tonya, and her affair with Yuri seems oddly truncated. Fated as they are to cross each other's paths (when they first touch, accidentally, on a trolley, Lean signals their mystic union with a spark from the trolley's overhead wire; again, we are reminded of a narrative presence), Yuri and Lara partake more of the metaphysical than the physical.

Here as elsewhere it could be argued that the confusions of Pasternak's novel nearly defeat the filmmakers; certainly, one sympathizes with their attempts to make sense of the novelist's ill-defined characters and simplistic thematics. Near the novel's end, Pasternak writes that Yuri and Lara "loved each other because everything around them willed it, the trees and the clouds and the sky over their heads and the earth under their feet."[9] It is easier to state this than to show it, and to state it as retrospective summary is easier still. Lean and Bolt attempt, perhaps mistakenly, to give this sentiment a visual pervasiveness. Their efforts are not uniformly rewarded with success, but it is difficult to see what else they could have done. As it is, the filmmakers succeed in creating an imagistic structure for the film, which, through evocations of wind, trees, flowers, and sky, associates Lara both with Yuri's mother, who dies when he is still a child and whose funeral on a windswept landscape begins the flashback, and to various aspects of the natural world. These associations are further emphasized by the balalaika that Yuri inherits from his mother and passes on to Lara and by Maurice Jarre's balalaika theme, which, initially associated with Yuri's mother, becomes the intimation of Lara's spirit and presence. Clearly, much of this imagery can be regarded as subjective, as Yuri's emotional coloring (Lean established Yuri's subjective—and hence "poetic"—vision at the outset when he shows Yuri visualizing his mother inside her closed coffin). Thus, when Lara leaves the makeshift hospital where she has come to know Yuri, the flower that begins to shed its petals is Yuri's flower (and, of course, Yevgref's, who is telling Yuri's story colored by his knowledge of Yuri's poetry), not Lean's.

The film's imagistic texture turns Lara into an emanation of nature, an earthy embodiment of "Life" (which is very much how Pasternak sees her), and at the same time idealizes and etherealizes her into an impossible projection of Yuri's overheated imagination. In neither role is she entirely convincing. For one thing, Julie Christie's 1960s look—wide eyes, teased blond hair, overripe lips—works against these symbolic concepts. But the major fault, it seems to me, is conceptual. Zhivago's yearning for Lara remains, within the definitions of his character, inexplicable, even perverse. Perhaps Lara and Tonya should be seen as two sides of Zhivago's personality, a split parallel to the one that presents him as sympathetic to human suffering but unable to embrace the revolution that proposes to rectify that suffering. But the relationship between the private and public worlds is uncertain (as in the novel, one must ask: If Lara is Life, what is Tonya?), and we are left with Zhivago's emotional self-indulgence made all the more questionable by the larger social/political issues that constantly interfere with his private happiness.

Lean's critique of romantic illusion evidences itself in his and Bolt's approach to politics as well. In Pasternak's *Doctor Zhivago*, the dialogue between public and private emerges as decidedly one-sided. The novelist sees Bolshevism as a failed god, an antilife force founded on a mechanistic philosophy that falsely seeks to elevate man above nature. To revolution he opposes the "joy of existence," a vague concept combining Christian mysticism and Russian nativism. Enthroning emotion above reason, Pasternak rejects the post-Enlightenment universe (Westerners, for some reason, tend to embrace this vision when expressed by a Pasternak or a Solzhenitsyn, evidently unaware that it implies a complete rejection of their way of life). Bolt and Lean construct a more dialectical foundation. Although Bolsheviks and other revolutionaries are frequently stereotyped in a manner that Pasternak's characters seldom are (indeed, some of the film's Russians look like refugees from *Ninotchka*), their politics is given its due. Or perhaps more than its due: revolutionary fervor, however wrong-headed, decidedly has the better of personal emotionalism. Some of the film's most interesting and involving characterizations are on the revolutionary side. Even a minor character like Razin (Noel William), the briefcase-carrying political officer attached to the partisans who kidnap Zhivago, retains considerable integrity even though required by the script to do and say unsympathetic things. Kostoyed, the anarchist forcefully played by Klaus Kinski, both anti-Bolshevik and antibourgeois, exhibits a passionate revolutionary spirit that cannot simply be credited to the Soviet side of the equation; nevertheless, his rough-edged intensity presents a radical alternative to "dubious poets" like Zhivago. Sasha/Strelnikov (Tom Courtenay), also a non-Bolshevik, an idealist betrayed by his own idealism, acts and suffers in a manner Lean clearly understands and with which he sympathizes. As at least one critic has noted, Strelnikov is the true Lean hero in *Doctor Zhivago.*[10] He belongs to that group of men (Colonel Nicholson, Lawrence) Lean had in the past made central to his films' concerns: fanatics who for an ideal drive themselves beyond good and evil.

Most interesting of all of the revolutionary characters, however, is Yuri's Bolshevik half-brother, Yevgref. Yuri's guardian angel in the novel, Pasternak's Yevgref has no life outside his symbolic functions. The first and last character we see in the film, the teller of the tale, he earns considerable audience identification. Neither a fanatic like Pasha nor passionate like Kostoyed, Yevgref, a practical revolutionary, believes in his cause and knows that some dirty work may be necessary to achieve it; he serves, in fact, in the secret police. Played by Alec Guinness with fine understatement, grace, and sardonic wit, Yevgref may be the film's most thoroughly likable character. A minor figure in his own narrative, he appears at key moments to save Yuri from himself, becoming at last the keeper of the flame, protector of Yuri's posthumous reputation. Furthermore, his voice-over narration, as is usual with this device, acquires a privileged status that sets the film's political tone. When Yevgref tells us, apropos of the outbreak of World War I, that "in bourgeois terms, it was a war between the Allies and Germany; in Bolshevik terms, it was a war between the Allied and German upper classes," we quite naturally share his evaluation. The subsequent montage depicting the horrors of war, wedded to Yevgref's narration, strongly upholds his credibility.

The revolution, in short, gathers to itself much of the film's dramatic energy, its validity further enhanced by contrast to the crassness, cynicism, and thoughtless materialism of the *ancien régime*. Although far from agit-prop, *Doctor Zhivago* presents a highly critical image of prerevolutionary Russia, a world of surface richness but little substance. Lean makes explicit the contrast between Russia's two worlds when he cross-cuts Lara's and Komarovsky's dinner party with the cossack massacre of demonstrators taking place on the street outside. Even a relatively benign character like Uncle Alex (Ralph Richardson), befuddled by the complexities of politics ("I wish they'd decide, once and for all, which gang of hooligans constitutes the government of this country"), cannot escape the myopia of the upper classes. Similarly, Tonya's self-indulgence (she returns from Paris early in the film with two groaning cartloads of suitcases and hatboxes), Professor Kurt's cynical worldliness, and Komarovsky's opportunism all undercut the czarist regime. The Bolsheviks may be harsh, small-minded, humorless, sometimes cruel bureaucrats, but they are allowed an integrity not evident in the aristocracy. Thus, the announcement of the czar's death, ostensibly a touching moment, actually lacks all resonance; the film has not established anything that would make us care.

Yuri Zhivago, the film's nominal hero, cannot redress the balance. A passive victim of historical forces, he seems ill-equipped to bear the standard for humane values. Zhivago does not act, he reacts. He sometimes behaves nobly, as when he runs a military hospital, sometimes ignobly, as when he begins an affair with Lara soon after settling his family at Varykino, but for the most part he is, as Lean was quite aware, an observer. "One of the most difficult things in *Zhivago*," Lean commented during the filming, "is the character of Zhivago himself, because he's not a typical screen hero. . . . He doesn't do anything, really; events happen around him, and this doesn't happen on the screen."[11] Lean compensates for this by time and again focusing on Zhivago's reaction to crucial events. The bloody cossack charge, for example, takes place on the soundtrack while we look at Yuri watching the massacre. This method, however, merely stresses Yuri's passivity; it does not transform it into action. Lean's film, for all of its rich, complex surface, its emotional power, and its enormous popularity (number 30 on *Variety*'s 1982 list of "All-Time Film Rental Champs"), too often seems a *Hamlet* without the Prince.

Ryan's Daughter (1970)

Ryan's Daughter contains the familiar ingredients of a surefire David Lean success: a love triangle; impressive scenery; social upheaval; Robert Bolt's dialogue; Freddie Young's cinematography; Maurice Jarre's music. And yet the film goes wildly, painfully awry. Though Lean provides us with a number of impressive moments—not the least being one of the most magnificent storm sequences ever filmed—these do not add up to a satisfactory cinematic experience. *Ryan's Daughter* fails massively and fundamentally; it fails in conception and in execution; it fails in outline and it fails in detail. What went wrong? Contemporary reviewers simply dismissed the film as overblown. But the problem, it seems to me, is not that simple. Although the film has no single, irredeemable flaw, it nevertheless exhibits a number of interconnected problems, most of which can be traced back to the elemental one of plot construction. And for this, Lean must bear full responsibility, even if Bolt wrote every word of the original screenplay. The story Lean and Bolt concocted rests on a fundamental misapprehension of the epic form. *Ryan's Daughter* has two subjects: Rosy Ryan's love affair and the Irish "troubles." Unfortunately, the two have virtually nothing to do with each other in the Lean/Bolt scenario.

For a love story set against the background of large human events to be compelling, two things at least are necessary: the lovers, whatever their errors and moral failings, must command our empathy, if not our entire sympathy; and, equally important, their individual fates must have some intimate link to the fate of the society they inhabit. In Tolstoy's *War and Peace*, to choose a classic example of a love story in epic form, we care about Natasha, Pierre, and Andre; we share their hopes, their desires, and their follies because they are at heart decent people and because their lives are profoundly affected by the political events in which they willingly or unwillingly participate. In a world undergoing cataclysmic changes, their concerns never seem merely trivial. *Ryan's Daughter* fails on both counts: we cannot care about the lovers nor do we find in their lives any connection with the world they inhabit.

Lean's lovers are surprisingly unappealing, and even his usual sympathy with the betrayed spouse misfires. Rosy Ryan, another of Lean's dissatisfied, yearning women, has not been sufficiently developed as a character to earn either our interest or our empathy. Bolt and Lean fail to make her predicament vivid and palpable. And the failure is compounded by casting. Sarah Miles, Bolt's wife at the time and the actress for whom he created the role, is completely miscast as Rosy: perhaps only a husband or a lover could have made such a grievous error. Miles does not transcend the sluttish persona that established her career (seducing Laurence Olivier in *Term of Trial*; helping to destroy James Fox in *The Servant*); as Rosy, a young girl awakening to the ecstasies of love, Miles works almost entirely against the grain of the character. And yet Rosy is the film's very center; if we cannot believe in her, little else matters. Nor does Rosy's lover inspire much interest. Conceived as a deeply flawed romantic figure, a kind of twentieth-century Heathcliff, Major Doryan, a handsome, shell-shocked, wounded hero/coward, is in fact only the outline of a character, with none of the details filled in. Christopher Jones looks beautifully right for the role, but he has no passion or charm. The triangle's third side,

Charles Shaughnessy, fares little better. No attempt is made to enter into his feelings, and the sympathy he automatically generates as a cuckold remains more mechanical than heartfelt. Robert Mitchum plays nobly against his screen image, but he seldom overcomes the script's limitations.

Remarkably, Bolt and Lean have failed to provide a single scene of the lovers in extended conversation. Physical passion is all very well, but lovers also talk; if nothing else, they talk about love. For the first time, Lean seems to have forgotten the difference between love and lust, a difference which, if it does not clearly manifest itself in life, is nevertheless indispensable in art. Ironically, the cinema's new license to speak frankly about sexual matters undermines Lean's kind of romantic love story. In films like *Brief Encounter, The Passionate Friends*, and even *Doctor Zhivago*, it was not necessary—or allowable—to discuss the sex lives of the characters. It was enough to suggest, for example, that Mary Justin (in *The Passionate Friends*) probably did not sleep with her husband (but, on the other hand, perhaps she did) and let it go at that. The adultery, in these earlier films, grew out of a complex of causes. A 1970 film, however, had to be more explicit, or so Lean must have thought. So he and Bolt construct an unappealing, embarrassing wedding-night sequence which clearly suggests that Charles (a middle-aged, but by no means old, widower) cannot satisfy Rosy's sexual wants. The whole episode is, frankly, preposterous. And the heightened romantic coloring in which the scenes between Rosy and Doryan are bathed seems equally foolish since the only issue at question, it would seem, is Rosy's orgasm. A woman's sexual dissatisfaction can, of course, be in itself a powerful theme, but neither Lean nor Bolt seem particularly interested in investigating Rosy's psyche to that extent. They clearly intend sex to be symbolic of other, less concrete emotions; unfortunately we never discover just what those other emotions are.

The weakness of the central love story would have mattered less had Lean and Bolt not isolated their protagonists from the social setting. Charles Shaughnessy has literally detached himself from the villagers and their concerns and he takes no part in the nationalist movement; Rosy, whose father (unknown to her) informs against his own people, never says a word or lifts a hand to help the Irish cause; and Major Doryan, the only one of the three directly involved in the political subplot, is not only on the "wrong" side but appears only marginally engaged, emotionally or intellectually, with what he is doing. What an extraordinary state of affairs! To see how extraordinary, one need merely imagine alternative scenarios. How very different, and how much more involving, the film would have been had either the husband or the lover been an IRA hero. What if Rosy had betrayed an Irish patriot to her lover, a British officer? Or what if Charles Shaughnessy had been the well-liked, respected schoolmaster whom Rosy deserts for Tim O'Leary, the IRA leader? In either case, the moral and political issues would have reflected and deepened each other.

Top: Robert Mitchum and Sarah Miles in Ryan's Daughter. *Bottom: Michael (John Mills) follows Major Doryan (Christopher Jones) in* Ryan's Daughter.

It may be objected that my scenarios are conventional Hollywood stuff compared to Bolt's more "realistic" treatment—after all, most people do stand aside from historical forces. What such an objection ignores, however, is that conventions are the blood and tissue of dramatic art, and that one deviates from them subtly and always at one's peril, not arbitrarily and foolishly. Bolt's plot may be more "realistic" than my imaginary ones, but it is not for realism primarily that we go to the movies.

Lean and Bolt's choice not to integrate their love story convincingly with the social and political background may have a very simple explanation: neither of them seems terribly sympathetic to Ireland or to the Irish cause. Lean has admitted that the choice of an Irish setting was more or less arbitrary ("It [the story] happens to be in Ireland, but I think it could happen anywhere"[12]), and the film demonstrates only too well the absence of an organic connection between story and setting. The Irish of *Ryan's Daughter,* certainly, are an unappealing lot. The fictional village of Kerry consists almost entirely of vulgar, unattractive girls, loutish boys, and their pinch-faced elders. Add a whiskey priest, a village idiot, and a loud-mouth publican (who is also an informer), and one can easily understand why Charles lives in an isolated schoolhouse some distance from the village. Lean and Bolt go overboard in stressing how much more refined than her peers Rosy is. Even Tim O'Leary, the IRA hero nicely played by Barry Foster, projects little in the way of warmth or charisma. In the film's very first sequence, significantly, O'Leary and his comrade shoot down an unarmed constable who they think may have recognized them; not exactly heroic behavior. All of this may point to a political statement—the Irish have been degraded by British rule—but it does so in a manner that does little credit to the Irish themselves, especially since the British soldiers are presented as generally sympathetic men who must make the best of a bad bargain. A seemingly incidental detail may best suggest where Lean and Bolt's sympathies lie: all during the storm sequence, "Mister" O'Keefe, the sinister-looking Sinn Finn operative—black raincoat, dark hat, steelrimmed glasses—sits in a truck while everyone else risks life and limb to salvage weapon shipments from the raging sea. So much for Irish nationalism.

Actually, it is only with the storm that the Irish cause comes to life at all. The entire sequence may be objectively unrealistic, but it is emotionally true and thematically valid: it has mythic scope. The villagers, in helping the IRA rescue its weapons, become energized. Cowards become heroes; loafers show unexpected courage; talkers become doers. Even the traitor, Ryan, risks his life, motivated as much by patriotism as by guilt. Plot and theme are here wed to the film's visual style as photography, music, performance, and editing all conspire to create epic, to capture the viewers' emotions. Ironically, it is precisely in this sequence that we are most aware of why the film does not work. The heroism, tension, and danger, the expression of enduring historical and natural forces here crystallized, cast into the shade the central romantic plot. None of the three major characters plays a role in the salvage, although Doryan arrives in time to capture both the guns and the outlaws. Traditionally, natural upheavals have symbolic resonance in the epic. One would expect Lean to project the storm as a macrocosmic echo of Rosy's passion. But no such connection emerges. The storm, however admirable as a piece of bravura filmmaking, becomes merely the main set-piece in a film that fails to integrate its various elements into a coherent whole. All of the sound and fury, alas, signify very little.

Lacking a firm center of gravity, *Ryan's Daughter* at its best can be little more than a series of ingenious set-pieces, intriguing bits floating around in a void. Symptomatically, the film's minor characters are more interesting than the major ones, at least in part because they are so much better cast. The priest, Father Hugh, gives Trevor Howard the opportunity for one of his best performances in years as he energizes a stereotypically conceived role with feeling detail. Leo McKern turns the traitor, Ryan, into a touching, pitiable figure. John Mills, whose performance could easily be dismissed as a tour de force, plays the idiot, Michael, with finely detailed pathos. If Michael is finally unconvincing as a character, it is not Mills's fault. The character has been burdened with symbolic overtones that point nowhere: he is a signifier without a signified. Much is made, for example, of Michael's identification with Major Doryan, but since the major is himself a virtually silent enigma, the point, if there is one, is lost.

And much the same applies to a number of the film's potentially interesting formal elements. The sequence where Shaughnessy imagines he can see the illicit lovers as he follows their tracks in the sand, for example, plays with the tension between objective and subjective (a favorite Lean motif), at one point combining the imaginary images of Rosy and Doryan in the same shot with the objectively real image of Charles, thus validating his fantasy. Impressive, too, is Lean's introduction of Doryan through Michael's eyes. As the bus bringing Doryan to Derry leaves the frame, we see his ramrod straight, impeccably tailored image silhouetted against the sky, a young god descended from Olympus. After a moment, he turns and walks off right, limping. The effect is breathtaking; an aura of mystery and magic envelops the lame hero. But, as the film does not generally seem to take Michael's point of view, the virtuosity of this sequence has finally little to which it can attach itself. That Doryan should be revealed as a deeply flawed man does not generate sufficient irony to justify such a grandiose introduction.

Ryan's Daughter demonstrates the limitations of the auteur theory, at least as it has been promulgated in this country. Lean here recapitulates many of the themes and situations of earlier films: a heroine (hero) uncomfortable in the world she (he) inhabits, yearning for something more and not even knowing (as Rosy says) "what more there is"; a backdrop of social upheaval; an adulterous love affair; tension between subjective and objective responses to the world; the failure of the romantic vision; the flawed military hero; landscape as character. All of this, nevertheless, fails to redeem the film. Lean tries almost too hard to construct an ideal Lean text without being able to provide the unifying energy that would make such a text valid. For Lean, the failure of *Ryan's Daughter* initiated a period of aborted projects followed by a premature retirement. For the whole series of roadshow epics that Lean himself had initiated with *Lawrence of Arabia*, *Ryan's Daughter*, following such other disasters as Robert Wise's *Star!* and Karel Reisz's *Isadora*, spelled the end. The giant, hard-ticket features that had been the film industry's answer to the threat from television had gone the way of the dinosaur. Already *The Poseidon Adventure* (directed by Ronald Neame, Lean's erstwhile Cineguild partner) was crowding them off the screen. The Seventies were to be the decade of the disaster movie, a tricky, unambiguous genre alien to Lean's concept of film.

But Lean's long period of silence may be coming to an end. In December, 1981, *Variety* announced a new David Lean project: an adaptation of E. M. Forster's novel *A Passage to India*. Once again, Lean would be exploring the subtle, complex human dimensions of imperialism. The production, moreover, would be British, returning Lean to his native context when we once again hear, following the critical acclaim and commercial success of *Chariots of Fire* and *Gandhi*, of a new "renaissance" in British films. Although other Lean projects have been announced and then dropped over the years, *A Passage to India* was still very much alive as late as November 1983. Lean, now seventy-five years old, was happily scouting locations, working on the script, and rounding up his cast (Alec Guinness, Peggy Ashcroft, Judy Davis, James Fox, and Victor Banerjee, among others). If all goes according to plan, David Lean may help to write a new, bright chapter in the checkered history of the British cinema.

Notes and References

Preface

1. Christian Metz, *Language and Cinema* (The Hague and Paris: Mouton, 1974), p. 76.

Chapter One

1. Marjorie Dent Candee, *Current Biography 1953* (New York: H. W. Wilson, 1954), p. 347.
2. *The British Film Industry* (London: Political & Economic Planning, 1952), p. 41.
3. Michael Chanan, *Labour Power in the British Film Industry* (London: British Film Institute, 1976), p. 23.
4. Michael Balcon et al., *Twenty Years of British Films 1925–1945* (London, 1947), p. 15.
5. Quoted in interview, *New York Times*, 9 November 1952, sect. 2, p. 5.
6. Ernest Betts, *The Film Business: A History of British Cinema 1896–1972* (London, 1973), p. 11.
7. Rachel Low, *The History of the British Film 1929–1939: Films of Comment and Persuasion of the 1930s* (London, 1979), p. 13.
8. Ibid., p. 13.
9. Interview with Howard Thompson, *New York Times*, 15 December 1957, sect. 2, p. 7.
10. James Holden, "'Best Technical Man in the Business': A Study of David Lean," *Film Journal* (Australia) 1 (April 1956):1.
11. Alan Wood, *Mr. Rank: A Study of J. Arthur Rank and British Films* (London, 1952), p. 131.

Chapter Two

1. Cited in Cole Lesley, *Remembered Laughter* (New York: Alfred A. Knopf, 1976), p. 215.

2. Richard de Rochemont, brother of *March of Time*'s Louis de Rochemont, observed in spring 1941: "For we Americans are an excessively violent people, and when we get confused and irritated we are likely to sock somebody in the jaw. We don't much care who it is. The nearest person, mostly. This is a definite *katharsis* for us, and we feel better after it. And we like to see others acting in the way that we consider normal. The films which have come from England have given Americans little emotional support in this respect. We have seen all types and conditions of men and men smiling amid inconceivable ruins. We have seen them do 'thumbs up.' We have heard them sing. And we feel, more and more, that if we were in the same boat we would not feel that way about it at all. And since we are beginning to climb into the boat with you, we wish you would act a little more the way we would." "As America Sees It," *Sight and Sound* 10 (Spring 1941):8.

3. *Time*, 28 December 1942, p. 84.

4. Bosley Crowther, *New York Times*, 24 December 1942, p. 18.

5. Gerald Pratley, *The Cinema of David Lean* (South Brunswick, N.J., and New York, 1974), pp. 31, 32.

6. Liz-Anne Bawden, ed., *The Oxford Companion to Film* (New York and London: Oxford University Press, 1976), p. 354.

7. Vincent Porter and Chaim Litewski, "*The Way Ahead*: Case History of a Propaganda Film," *Sight and Sound* 50 (Spring 1981):110–16; 111.

8. Arthur Marwick, *The Explosion of British Society 1914–1970*, 2d ed. (London: Macmillan, 1971), p. 98. Cited in Roy Armes, *A Critical History of the British Cinema* (New York, 1978), p. 145.

9. Lindsay Anderson, "Get Out and Push!," in Tom Maschler, ed., *Declaration* (New York: E. P. Dutton, 1958), p. 140.

10. Leif Furhammar and Folke Isaksson, *Politics and Film*, trans. Kersti French (New York: Praeger, 1971), p. 192.

11. George Perry, *The Great British Picture Show* (New York, 1974), p. 108.

12. Edward Branigan, "The Spectator and Film Space—Two Theories," *Screen* 22 (1981):61.

13. Douglas McVay, "Lean—Lover of Life," *Films and Filming* 5 (August 1959):9.

14. Manny Farber, review, *New Republic* 113 (23 October 1945):573.

Chapter Three

1. Leo Braudy, *The World in a Frame* (New York: Anchor Press, 1977), p. 46.

2. "Brief Encounter," in *Masterworks of the British Cinema*, intro. John Russell Taylor (New York: Harper & Row, 1974), p. 79.

3. For a discussion of the music in *Brief Encounter* that closely parallels mine, see A. R. Fulton, *Motion Pictures* (Norman, Okla., 1960; rev. 1980), pp. 179–80.

4. Raymond Durgnat, *A Mirror for England* (London, 1970), p. 180.

5. Perry, *Great British Picture Show*, p. 17.

6. John Ellis, "Art, Culture and Quality—Terms for a Cinema in the Forties and Seventies," *Screen* 19 (Autumn 1978):9–49; 15.

Chapter Four

1. Peter Forster, "J. Arthur Rank and the Shrinking Screen" in *Age of Austerity*, ed. Philip French and Michael Sissons (London: Hodden & Stoughton, 1963).

2. Richard Winnington, *Film: Criticism and Caricatures 1943–53* (New York: Barnes and Noble, 1976), p. 171.

3. Ibid, pp. 82–83.

4. Charles Dickens, *Great Expectations*, intro. Frederick Page (London: Oxford University Press, 1953), p. 101.

5. K. J. Fielding, *Charles Dickens: A Critical Introduction* (New York: David McKay, 1958), p. 179.

6. Metz, *Language and Cinema*, p. 16.

7. Roland Barthes, *S/Z*, trans. Richard Miller (New York: Hill & Wang, 1974), p. 80.

8. Dickens, *Great Expectations*, pp. 1–2.

9. These are described and illustrated with frame enlargements in Karel Reisz's *The Technique of Film Editing* (London, 1953), pp. 237–41.

10. Ibid., p. 240.

11. For an excellent discussion of Lean's ending, see Alain Silver, "The Untranquil Light: David Lean's *Great Expectations*," *Literature/Film Quarterly* 2 (Spring 1974):140–52.

12. Dickens, *Great Expectations*, p. 219.

13. Dorothy Van Ghent, *The English Novel: Form and Function* (New York: Rinehart & Co., 1953), p. 134.

14. For a somewhat different view of the class implications of *Great Expectations*, see Durgnat, *Mirror for England*, pp. 21–23.

15. Sergei Eisenstein, "Dickens, Griffith, and the Film Today," in *Film Form* (New York, 1949), pp. 195–255.

16. Arnold Kettle, *An Introduction to the English Novel* (London: Hutchinson & Co., Ltd., 1951; rev. ed., New York: Harper & Row, 1967), p. 121.

17. J. Hillis Miller, "The Fiction of Realism: *Sketches by Boz, Oliver Twist*, and Cruikshank's Illustrations," in *Charles Dickens and George Cruikshank* (Los Angeles: William Andrews Clark Memorial Library, University of California, 1971), p. 44.

18. Cited in ibid.

19. David Bordwell, *The Films of Carl-Theodore Dreyer* (Berkeley: University of California Press, 1981), p. 81.

20. J. Hillis Miller, *Charles Dickens: The World of His Novels* (Cambridge, Mass.: Harvard University Press, 1958), p. 43.

21. Eisenstein, "Dickens . . . ," pp. 206, 208, 217.

22. Charles Dickens, *Oliver Twist* (New York: New American Library, 1961), p. 36.

23. Dickens, *Oliver Twist*, p. 87.

24. "Brief Encounter," *Penguin Film Review* 4 (London, 1947): 35.

Chapter Five

1. Perry, *Great British Picture Show*, p. 140.

2. Karol Kulik, *Alexander Korda* (London: W. H. Allen, 1975), p. 311.

3. Ron Pickard, "David Lean, Supreme Craftsman," *Films in Review* 25 (May 1974):275.

4. Tom Wolfe's chronicle of the Mercury space project includes an amusing account of Chuck Yeager's response to Lean's film; it was Yeager, an American, who first broke the sound barrier. See *The Right Stuff* (New York: Farrar, Straus, Giroux, 1979), pp. 61–62.

5. Michael Balcon, "10 Years of British Films," *Films in 1951: Festival of Britain* (London: British Film Institute, 1951), p. 37.

Chapter Six

1. One might compare an earlier Katharine Hepburn film, *Christopher Strong* (Dorothy Arzner, 1933). In that film, Lady Cynthia Darlington (!) is introduced to us quite explicitly as a virgin. Her celibacy, however, is chosen; she has better use for her time and energy (of course, she is also very young, which makes a difference).

2. John Sproas, *The Decline of the Cinema* (London: George Allen & Unwin, 1962), p. 22.

3. The American Film Institute library owns a copy of what is very likely Foreman's draft, though—like other extant scripts of the film—it is credited to Pierre Boulle.

4. Pierre Boulle, *The Bridge Over the River Kwai*, trans. Xan Fielding (New York: Vanguard Press, 1954), p. 27.

5. Armes, *Critical History*, p. 213.

6. Alan Sked and Chris Cook, *Post-War Britain* (Sussex: Harvester Press, 1979), p. 146.

7. Ibid., p. 153.

8. Ian Watt, "Bridges Over the Kwai," *Partisan Review* 26 (Winter 1959):83–94; 89.

Chapter Seven

1. Cited in Phillip Knightley and Colin Simpson, *The Secret Lives of Lawrence of Arabia* (New York: McGraw-Hill, 1969), p. 155.

2. In *T. E. Lawrence by His Friends*, ed. A. W. Lawrence (Abridged ed., New York: Doubleday, 1954; New York: Doubleday, 1937), p. 382.

3. Cited in Samuel Hynes, *The Auden Generation* (New York: Viking Press, 1977), p. 191.

4. T. E. Lawrence, *Seven Pillars of Wisdom* (Garden City, N.Y: Doubleday Doran, 1937), pp. 445, 447.

5. Ibid., p. 562.

6. Edward Said, *Orientalism* (New York: Pantheon Books, 1978), pp. 63, 71–72.

7. Joseph Campbell, *The Hero With a Thousand Faces*, 2d ed. (Princeton, N.J.; Princeton University Press, 1968), p. 29.

Chapter Eight

1. Edmund Wilson, "Doctor Life and His Guardian Angel," in *The Bit Between My Teeth* (New York: Farrar, Straus & Giroux, 1965), p. 446.

2. Robert Bolt, *Doctor Zhivago: The Screenplay* (New York: Random House, 1965), pp. xv–xvi.

3. Ibid., p. xv.

4. Boris Pasternak, *Doctor Zhivago*, trans. Max Hayward and Manya Harari (New York: Pantheon Books, 1958), p. 144.

5. Ibid., p. 236.

6. Ibid., pp. 286–87.

7. Ibid., p. 69.

8. Ibid., pp. 70–71.

9. Ibid., p. 417.

10. Steven Ross, "In Defense of David Lean," *Take One* 3 (July-August 1972):10–18; 17.

11. R. S. Stewart, "Doctor Zhivago: The Making of a Movie," *Atlantic Monthly* 216 (August 1965):58–64; 60.

12. Pratley, *Cinema of David Lean*, p. 204.

Selected Bibliography

1. Books

ARMES, ROY. *A Critical History of the British Cinema.* New York: Oxford University Press, 1978. The best one-volume survey, though not as "critical" or rigorously analytic as its title seems to promise.

BALCON, MICHAEL, et al. *Twenty Years of British Films: 1925–1945.* London: The Falcon Press Ltd., 1947. Essays by Michael Balcon, Ernest Lindgren, Forsyth Hardy, and Roger Manvell assessing the immediate past history of the British cinema with (justifiable) pride and (less justifiably) looking forward to an equally productive future.

BETTS, ERNEST. *The Film Business: A History of British Cinema 1896–1972.* London: George Allen & Unwin, 1973. A somewhat pedestrian history of the British cinema, which as its title indicates "concentrates on the business aspect of British films, and specifically on the twin evils of government interference and American influence."

The British Film Industry. London: Political & Economic Planning, 1952. A careful, detailed study of the British cinema considered primarily as a business, concentrating on the situation of the industry at the beginning of the 1950s but including a solid though brief economic history of British films.

CASTELLI, LOUIS P., with CLEELAND, CARYN LYNN. *David Lean: A Guide to References and Resources.* Boston: G. K. Hall, 1980. Although it suffers from errors and omissions, this is the most comprehensive source of information available to anyone interested in David Lean; particularly useful are the Annotated Guide to Writings About David Lean and the list of Archival Sources.

DURGNAT, RAYMOND. *A Mirror For England.* London: Faber & Faber, 1970. A quirky, highly opinionated, but nearly always fascinating account of British films from the 1940s to the 1960s.

FULTON, A. R. *Motion Pictures: The Development of an Art.* Norman: University of Oklahoma Press, 1980. First published in 1960, and therefore one of the earliest of film "textbooks," *Motion Pictures* contains thorough, detailed discussions of *Brief Encounter* and *Great Expectations* treated primarily as adaptations that suffer somewhat from an unsophisticated view of the concept "cinematic."

LOW, RACHEL. *The History of the British Film 1929–1939: Films of Comment and Persuasion of the 1930s.* London: George Allen & Unwin, 1979. A survey of the British newsreel and nonfiction propaganda films of the period; helpful background for Lean's newsreel period.

PERRY, GEORGE. *The Great British Picture Show*. New York: Hill & Wang, 1974. A lively, popular history of British films that artfully arranges a good deal of valuable information.

PRATLEY, GERALD. *The Cinema of David Lean*. South Brunswick, N.J., and New York: A. S. Barnes & Co., 1974. A careful collection of Lean's credits, supplemented with synopses of each film, excerpts from interviews, and a general, unanalytical commentary.

REISZ, KAREL. *The Technique of Film Editing*. London: The Focal Press, 1953. A general survey and handbook of British and American editing strategies that includes detailed analyses, with frame enlargements, of sequences from *Great Expectations* and *The Passionate Friends*.

SILVER, ALAIN, and URSINI, JAMES. *David Lean and His Films*. London: Leslie Frewin, 1974. An excellent critical study of Lean's films from an unabashedly auteurist viewpoint, beautifully illustrated throughout.

WOOD, ALAN. *Mr. Rank: A Study of J. Arthur Rank and British Films*. London: Hodder & Stoughton, 1952. Much more than a biography of one of the major forces in the British cinema, this book offers knowledgeable insight into the workings of the entire British industry from the 1930s to the 1950s.

2. Articles and Parts of Books

CRABBE, KATHARYN. "Lean's *Oliver Twist:* Novel to Film." *Film Criticism* 2 (Fall 1977): 46–51. A brief but suggestive analysis of *Oliver Twist* that argues that Lean, by employing the customary adaptive strategies of simplification, expansion, and substitution, transforms the realism and irony of Dickens into his own brand of fantasy and romance.

"David Lean Talks to Roger Manvell." In Roger Manvell and R. K. Neilson Baxter, eds. *The Cinema 1952*. London: Penguin Books, 1952, pp. 19–20. Brief comments by Lean on the making of *Great Expectations* followed by an extract from the film's post-production script.

FARBER, STEPHEN. "Lean and Lawrence: The Last Adventurers." In *Favorite Movies*. Edited by Philip Nobile. New York: Macmillan, 1973. An excellent, highly enthusiastic appreciation of *Lawrence of Arabia* as "one of the last great works in straight-line dramatic cinema."

GEDULD, HARRY M., ed. *Film Makers on Film Making*. Bloomington and London: Indiana University Press, 1967. Includes a chapter, "The Film Maker and the Audience," which extracts portions of a questionnaire and the responses to it by a group of directors, including Lean, who gives his opinion on censorship (problems with *Oliver Twist*) as well as encouraging and discouraging developments in the film industry.

HOLDEN, JAMES. "'Best Technical Man in the Business': A Study of David Lean." *Film Journal* 1 (April 1956):1–5. An early negative estimate that acknowledges Lean's technical mastery while regretting his "refusal to commit himself to a positive attitude to his theme[s]" and concluding that Lean is "capable of importing to his films only a brilliant surface gloss."

HUNTLEY, JOHN. "The Music of 'Hamlet' and 'Oliver Twist.'" *Penguin Film Review* 8 (1949):110–22. Includes excerpts from notes made by Lean as directions to Sir Arnold Bax, who composed the music for *Oliver Twist*.

JOYAUX, GEORGES. "*The Bridge Over the River Kwai*: From the Novel to the Movie." *Literature/Film Quarterly* 2 (Spring 1974):174–82. Considers the changes between Boulle's novel and Lean's film and in particular the "compromises" that were made in order to satisfy the tastes of a mass audience.

LEAN, DAVID. "Brief Encounter." *Penguin Film Review* 4 (1947):27–35. In this somewhat misleadingly titled but very informative essay, Lean discusses the "new realism" of the postwar British cinema, which has helped to make British films more popular than Hollywood films in Great Britain, and traces the history of Independent Producers, Inc., which Lean sees as largely responsible for the new vitality evident in the British film industry.

———. "The Film Director." In *Working for the Films*. Edited by Oswell Blakeston. London: The Focal Press, 1947, pp. 27–37. A fairly straightforward view of the directing process, of interest primarily in the emphasis Lean places on editing and in his statement that "the best films are generally those that have the stamp of one man's personality."

———. "Out of the Wilderness." *Films and Filming* 9 (January 1963):12–15. An interview in the form of an article in which Lean discusses the genesis, preproduction, and filming of *Lawrence of Arabia*.

MCVAY, DOUGLAS. "Lean—Lover of Life." *Films and Filming* 5 (August 1959):9–10, 34. One of the best essays on Lean's career: carefully researched, balanced in its critical estimates, and generally sympathetic even if the final judgment that Lean "may exhibit no consistently personal style and attitude toward life" greatly qualifies the earlier enthusiasm.

MOYNAHAN, JULIAN. "Seeing the Book, Reading the Movie." In *The English Novel and the Movies*. Edited by Michael Klein and Gillian Parker. New York: Frederick Ungar, 1981, pp. 143–54. A somewhat self-indulgent, sketchy essay on *Great Expectations* as novel and film. Praises Lean for a number of fine "touches" but faults him for the ending and for eliminating a number of subsidiary characters.

PICKARD, RON. "David Lean: Supreme Craftsman." *Films in Review* 25 (May 1974):265–84. A useful survey of Lean's career that quotes frequently from an interview with Lean and includes a good deal of background information and a filmography.

PRICE, STANLEY. "On the Spanish Steppes with Dr. Zhivago." *Show* 5 (May 1965):36–41. Background information on the filming of *Dr. Zhivago* in Spain, with excerpts from interviews with Lean and members of his cast and crew interwoven with a slight survey of Lean's career and methods.

REYNOLDS, CHARLES. "What You Can Learn from Movies." *Popular Photography* 42 (March 1958):108–9, 115. A rather slight interview-article, illustrated with stills and frame enlargements from *Bridge on the River Kwai*, in which Lean gives advice to the amateur photographer on such matters as lighting and composition.

ROSS, STEVEN. "In Defense of David Lean." *Take One* 3 (July-August 1972):10–18. An important, spirited reevaluation of Lean's films that stresses the director's "consistently tragic vision of the romantic sensibility attempting to reach beyond the restraints and constrictions of everyday life."

SARRIS, ANDREW. *Interviews with Film Directors*. New York: Avon, 1967. Includes an interview with Lean, conducted by Gerald Pratley, emphasizing *Dr. Zhivago* and Lean's collaboration with writers.

SILVER, ALAIN. "The Untranquil Light: David Lean's *Great Expectations.*" *Literature/Film Quarterly* 2 (Spring 1974):140–52. A careful discussion of Lean's adaptive strategies, featuring an excellent analysis of his much-maligned solution to the problem of how to end the film. Substantially reprinted in Silver and Ursini (see above, under Books).

STEWART, R. S. "*Doctor Zhivago*: The Making of a Movie." *Atlantic Monthly* 216 (August 1965):58–64. An extremely useful article for an understanding of Lean's working methods, comprised mainly of interviews with Lean, Omar Sharif, and Robert Bolt.

THOMPSON, HOWARD. "Career Inventory from the Lean Viewpoint." *New York Times*, 9 November 1952, sect. 2, p. 5. An interview-article in which Lean discusses his early years in the film business and his approach to adapting Dickens.

YOUNG, VERNON. "Dickens without Holly: David Lean's *Oliver Twist.*" *New Mexico Quarterly* 22 (1952): 425–30. In this highly laudatory analysis of Lean's film, Vernon Young finds that Lean has surpassed not only most Hollywood filmmakers but even Dickens himself.

WATT, IAN. "Bridges Over the Kwai." *Partisan Review* 26 (Winter 1959):83–94. An intriguing discussion of Lean's film, Boulle's novel, and the historical realities that lie behind both, by a distinguished literary critic who was a British POW in Burma when the "real" bridge was built.

ZAMBRANO, A. L. "*Great Expectations*: Dickens and David Lean." *Literature/Film Quarterly* 2 (Spring 1974):154–61. An article that stresses the fairy-tale atmosphere of Lean's adaptation, citing passages from the original shooting script to illustrate significant points.

3. Film

David Lean: A Self-Portrait. Produced and directed by Thomas Craven. Pyramid Films, 1971 (59 minutes). An excellent film interview with Lean interspersed with clips from his major films, location footage from *Lawrence of Arabia, Dr. Zhivago*, and *Ryan's Daughter*, and interviews with Lean associates Robert Bolt, Sam Spiegel, Anthony Havelock-Allan, and Freddie Young. Lean discusses working on the script, editing, and location filming, as well as his attitudes toward critics and the public.

Filmography

IN WHICH WE SERVE (British Lion/United Artists, 1942)
Producer: Noel Coward
Associate Producer: Anthony Havelock-Allen
Co-Director: Noel Coward
Screenplay: Noel Coward
Cinematographer: Ronald Neame
Art Director: David Rawnsley
Art Supervisor (to Noel Coward): G. E. Calthrop
Music: Noel Coward
Sound: C. C. Stevens
Editors: David Lean and Thelma Myers
Cast: Noel Coward (Captain "D" Kinross), Bernard Miles (Chief Petty Officer Walter Hardy), John Mills (Ordinary Seaman Shorty Blake), Celia Johnson (Mrs. Kinross), Kay Walsh (Freda Lewis), Joyce Carey (Mrs. Hardy), Derek Elphinstone (Number One), Robert Sansom ("Guns"), Philip Friend ("Torps"), Michael Wilding ("Flags"), Hubert Gregg (Pilot), Ballard Berkeley (Engineer Commander), James Donald (Doctor), Kathleen Harrison (Mrs. Blake), George Carney (Mr. Blake), Richard Attenborough (Young Sailor), Daniel Massey (Bobby), Juliet Mills (Freda's baby)
Running time: 113 (or 115) minutes
Premier: 1 October 1942
16mm rental: Kit Parker Films

THIS HAPPY BREED (Eagle Lion/Universal International, 1944)
Producer: Noel Coward
Associate Producer: Anthony Havelock-Allen
Assistant Director: George Pollock
Screenplay: Noel Coward, from his play
Cinematographer: Ronald Neame (Technicolor)
Special Effects: Percy Day
Art Director: C. P. Norman
Art Supervisor (to Noel Coward): G. E. Calthrop
Dress Supervisor: Hilda Collins
Musical Director: Muir Matheson
Sound: C. C. Stevens, John Cooke, Desmond Drew

Editor: Jack Harris
Cast: Robert Newton (Frank Gibbons), Celia Johnson (Ethel Gibbons), Amy Veness (Mrs. Flint), Alison Leggatt (Aunt Sylvia), Stanley Holloway (Bob Mitchell), John Mills (Billy Mitchell), Kay Walsh (Queenie Gibbons), Eileen Erskine (Vi Gibbons), John Blythe (Reg Gibbons), Guy Verney (Sam Leadbitter), Betty Fleetwood (Phyllis Blake), Merle Tottenham (Edie)
Running time: 111 (or 107) minutes
Premier: June 1944 (Great Britain); April 1947 (United States)
16mm rental: Janus Films

BLITHE SPIRIT (General Film Distributors/United Artists, 1945)
Producer: Noel Coward
Associate Producer: Anthony Havelock-Allen
Assistant Director: George Pollock
Screenplay: Noel Coward, from his play
Adaptation: David Lean, Ronald Neame, Anthony Havelock-Allen
Cinematographer: Ronald Neame
Special Effects: Tom Howard
Art Director: C. P. Norman
Art Supervisor (to Noel Coward): G. E. Calthrop
Costumes: Rahvia
Music: Richard Addinsell
Sound: John Cooke, Desmond Drew
Editor: Jack Harris
Cast: Rex Harrison (Charles Condomine), Constance Cummings (Ruth), Kay Hammond (Elvira), Margaret Rutherford (Madame Arcati), Joyce Carey (Mrs. Bradman), Hugh Wakefield (Doctor Bradman), Jacqueline Clark (Edith)
Running time: 96 minutes
Premier: April 1945 (Great Britain); September 1945 (United States)
16mm rental: Images; Budget

BRIEF ENCOUNTER (Eagle Lion/Universal International, 1945)
Producer: Noel Coward
Associate Producers: Anthony Havelock-Allen and Ronald Neame
Assistant Director: George Pollock
Screenplay: David Lean, Ronald Neame, and Anthony Havelock-Allen, from Noel Coward's play "Still Life" from *Tonight at 8:30*
Adaptation: Noel Coward
Cinematographer: Robert Krasker
Art Director: L. P. Williams
Art Supervisor (to Noel Coward): G. E. Calthrop
Music: Rachmaninoff's Piano Concerto No. 2 played by Eileen Joyce, with the National Symphony Orchestra conducted by Muir Mathieson
Sound: Stanley Lambourne and Desmond Drew
Editor: Jack Harris
Associate Editor: Harry Miller

Cast: Celia Johnson (Laura Jesson), Trevor Howard (Dr. Alec Harvey), Cyril Raymond (Fred Jesson), Stanley Holloway (Albert Godby), Joyce Carey (Myrtle Baggot), Margaret Barton (Beryl Waters), Valentine Dyall (Stephen Lynn), Everley Gregg (Dolly Messiter), Marjorie Mars (Mary Norton), Jack May (Boatman)
Running Time: 86 minutes
Premier: November 1945 (Great Britain); August 1946 (United States)
16mm rental: Images; Budget

GREAT EXPECTATIONS (General Film Distributors/Universal International, 1946)
Producer: Ronald Neame
Executive Producer: Anthony Havelock-Allen
Assistant Director: George Pollock
Screenplay: David Lean, Ronald Neame, Anthony Havelock-Allen, with Kay Walsh and Cecil McGivern, adapted from the book by Charles Dickens
Cinematographer: Guy Green
Production Designer: John Bryan
Art Director: Wilfred Shingleton
Costumes: Sophia Harris (of Motley) assisted by Margaret Furse
Music: Walter Goehr (Kenneth Pakeman, G. Linley, uncredited)
Sound: Stanley Lambourne and Gordon K. McCullum (Desmond Drew, uncredited)
Sound Editor: Winston Ryder
Editor: Jack Harris
Cast: John Mills (Pip, grown up), Valerie Hobson (Estella, grown up), Bernard Miles (Joe Gargery), Francis L. Sullivan (Jaggers), Finlay Currie (Magwitch), Martita Hunt (Miss Havisham), Anthony Wager (Pip, as a boy), Jean Simmons (Estella, as a girl), Alec Guinness (Herbert Pocket), John Forrest (Pale Young Gentleman), Ivor Barnard (Wemmick), Freda Jackson (Mrs. Joe Gargery), Torin Thatcher (Bentley Drummle), Eileen Erskine (Biddy), Hay Petrie (Uncle Pumblechook), George Hayes (Compeyson, the other convict), Richard George (The Sergeant), Everly Gregg (Sarah Pocket), O. B. Clarence (The Aged Parent), John Burch (Mr. Wopsle)
Running time: 118 (or 115 minutes)
Premier: December 1946 (Great Britain); April 1947 (United States)
16mm rental: Images; Budget

OLIVER TWIST (Eagle Lion/United Artists, 1948)
Producer: Ronald Neame
Assistant Director: George Pollock
Screenplay: David Lean and Stanley Haynes, adapted from the book by Charles Dickens
Cinematographer: Guy Green
Special Effects: Joan Suttie and Stanley Grant
Art Director: John Bryan
Costumes: Margaret Furse
Makeup: Stuart Freebourne
Music: Sir Arnold Bax

Sound: Stanley Lambourne and Gordon K. McCallum
Sound Editor: Winston Ryder
Editor: Jack Harris
Cast: Robert Newton (Bill Sikes), Alec Guinness (Fagin), Kay Walsh (Nancy), Francis L. Sullivan (Mr. Bumble), Henry Stephenson (Mr. Brownlow), Mary Clare (Mrs. Corney), John Howard Davies (Oliver Twist), Josephine Stuart (Oliver's Mother), Henry Edwards (Police Official), Ralph Truman (Monks), Anthony Newly (The Artful Dodger), Kenneth Downy (Workhouse Master), Gibb McLaughlin (Mr. Sowerberry), Kathleen Harrison (Mrs. Sowerberry), Amy Veness (Mrs. Bedwin), W. G. Fay (Bookseller), Maurice Denham (Chief of Police), Frederick Lloyd (Mr. Grimwig), Ivor Barnard (Chairman of the Board), Deirdre Doyle (Mrs. Thingummy), Diana Dors (Charlotte), Michael Dear (Noah Claypole), Peter Bull (Landlord of the "Three Cripples")
Running time: 116 minutes (104 minutes, U.S. release)
Premier: June 1948 (Great Britain); July 1951 (United States)
16mm rental: Janus

THE PASSIONATE FRIENDS (U.S. title: **ONE WOMAN'S STORY**) (General Film Distributors/Universal International, 1949)
Producer: Ronald Neame
Associate Producer: Norman Spencer
Assistant Director: George Pollock
Screenplay: Eric Ambler, based on the novel by H. G. Wells
Adaptation: David Lean and Stanley Haynes
Cinematographer: Guy Green
Art Director: John Bryan
Assistant Art Director: Tim Hopwell-Ashe
Set Decorator: Claude Manusey
Costumes: Margaret Furse
Music: Richard Addinsell
Sound: Stanley Lambourne and Gordon K. McCallum
Sound Editor: Winston Ryder
Editor: Geoffrey Foot
Cast: Ann Todd (Mary Justin), Claude Rains (Howard Justin), Trevor Howard (Steven Stratton), Isabel Dean (Pat), Betty Ann Davies (Miss Layton), Arthur Howard (Servant), Guide Lorraine (Hotel Manager), Natasha Sikolova (Chambermaid), Helen Burls (Flower-woman)
Running time: 87 (or 91) minutes
Premier: January 1949 (Great Britain); June 1949 (United States)
16mm rental: none

MADELEINE (General Film Distributors/Walter Reade and Universal International, 1950)
Producer: Stanley Haynes
Assistant Director: George Pollock
Screenplay: Stanley Haynes and Nicholas Phipps, based on the case of Madeleine Hamilton Smith
Cinematographer: Guy Green

Art Director: John Bryan
Costumes: Margaret Furse
Music: William Alwyn
Editor: Geoffrey Foot
Cast: Ann Todd (Madeleine Smith), Ivan Desny (Emile L'Angelier), Norman Wooland (Mr. Minnoch), Leslie Banks (Mr. Smith), Barbara Everest (Mrs. Smith), Susan Stranks (Janet Smith), Patricia Raine (Bessie Smith), Elizabeth Sellars (Christina), Edward Chapman (Dr. Thompson), Jean Cadell (Mrs. Jenkins), Eugene Deckers (Monsieur Thuau), Ivor Barnard (Mr. Murdoch), Harry Jones (Lord Advocate), David Horne (Lord Justice), Andre Morell (Dean of Faculty), Amy Veness (Miss Aiken), John Laurie (Scots Divine), James McKechine (Narrator)
Running time: 114 minutes
Premier: February 1950 (Great Britain); September 1950 (United States)
16mm rental: Budget; Kit Parker Films

THE SOUND BARRIER (British Lion/Lopert Films—United Artists, 1950) (alternate titles: **BREAKING THROUGH THE SOUND BARRIER** [Great Britain and United States]; **BREAKING THE SOUND BARRIER** [United States])
Producer: David Lean
Associate Producer: Norman Spencer
Aerial Unit Director: Anthony Squire
Screenplay: Terence Rattigan
Cinematographer: Jack Hildyard
Aerial Unit Cinematography: John Wilcox, Jo Jago, Peter Newbrook
Art Directors: Vincent Korda, Joseph Bato, John Hawkesworth
Music: Malcolm Arnold
Editor: Geoffrey Foot
Cast: Ralph Richardson (Sir John Ridgefield), Ann Todd (Susan Ridgefield Garthwaite), Nigel Patrick (Tony Garthwaite), John Justin (Philip Peel), Dinah Sheridan (Jess Peel), Joseph Tomelty (Will Sparks), Denholm Elliot (Christopher Ridgefield), Jack Allen (Windy Williams), Ralph Michael (Fletcher)
Running time: 118 minutes
Premier: July 1952 (Great Britain); November 1952 (United States)
16mm rental: Select Films

HOBSON'S CHOICE (British Lion/United Artists, 1954)
Producer: David Lean
Associate Producer: Norman Spencer
Assistant Director: Adrian Pryce-Jones
Screenplay: David Lean, Norman Spencer, and Wynyard Browne, from the play by Harold Brighouse
Cinematographer: Jack Hildyard
Art Director: Wilfred Shingleton
Costumes: John Armstrong, Julia Squire
Music: Malcolm Arnold
Sound: John Cox
Sound Recording: Buster Ambler and Red Law

Editor: Peter Taylor
Cast: Charles Laughton (Henry Hobson), John Mills (William Mossop), Brenda de Banzie (Maggie Hobson), Daphne Anderson (Alice Hobson), Prunella Scales (Vicky Hobson), Richard Wattis (Albert Prosser), Derek Blomfield (Freddy Beenstock), Helen Haye (Mrs. Hepworth), Joseph Tomelty (Jim Heeler), Julian Mitchell (Sam Minns), Gibb McLaughlin (Tudsbury), John Laurie (Dr. McFarlane)
Running time: 107 minutes
Premier: February 1954 (Great Britain); June 1954 (United States)
16mm rental: Janus

SUMMER MADNESS (U.S. title: **SUMMERTIME**) (Independent—British Lion/United Artists, 1955)
Producer: Ilya Lopert
Associate Producer: Norman Spencer
Assistant Directors: Adrian Pryce-Jones, Alberto Cardone
Screenplay: H. E. Bates and David Lean, from the play *The Time of the Cuckoo* by Arthur Laurents
Cinematographer: Jack Hildyard (Technicolor)
Production Designer: Vincent Korda
Art Directors: Bill Hutchinson, Ferdinane Bellan
Music: Alessandro Cicognini; Rossini's "La Gazza Ladra"
Sound: Peter Hanford, John Cox
Editor: Peter Taylor
Cast: Katharine Hepburn (Jane Hudson), Rossano Brazzi (Renato De Rossi), Isa Miranda (Signora Fiorini), Darren McGavin (Eddie Jaeger), Mari Aldon (Phyllis Jaeger), Jane Rose (Mrs. Edith McIlhenny), MacDonald Parke (Lloyd McIlhenny), Gaetano Autiero (Mauro), Andre Morell (Englishman on train), Jeremy Spenser (Vito), Virginia Simeon (Giovanna)
Running time: 100 minutes
Premier: May 1955 (Great Britain); June 1955 (United States)
16mm rental: Budget; Kit Parker Films

THE BRIDGE ON THE RIVER KWAI (Columbia, 1957)
Producer: Sam Spiegel
Assistant Directors: Gus Agosti; Ted Sturgis
Screenplay: Pierre Boulle (Carl Foreman, Michael Wilson, uncredited), from his novel
Cinematographer: Jack Hildyard (Technicolor; CinemaScope)
Art Director: Donald M. Ashton
Technical Advisor: Major-General L. E. M. Perowne
Music: Malcolm Arnold
Sound: John Cox and John Mitchell
Chief Sound Editor: Winston Ryder
Editor: Peter Taylor
Cast: William Holden (Shears), Alec Guinness (Col. Nicholson), Jack Hawkins (Major Warden), Sessue Hayakawa (Colonel Saito), James Donald (Major Clipton), Geoffrey Horne (Lieutenant Joyce), Andre Morell (Colonel Green),

Peter Williams (Captain Reeves), John Boxer (Major Hughes), Percy Herbert (Grogan), Harold Goodwin (Baker), Ann Sears (Nurse), Henry Okawa (Captain Kanematsu), Keiichiro Katsumoto (Lieutenant Miura), M. R. B. Chakrabandhu (Yai), Vilaiwan Seeboonreaung, Ngamta Suphaphongs, Javanart Punynchoti, Kannikar Dowklee (Siamese girls)
Running time: 161 minutes
Premier: November 1957
16mm rental: Images; Kit Parker Films

LAWRENCE OF ARABIA (Columbia, 1962)
Producer: Sam Spiegel
Assistant Director: Roy Stevens
Second Unit Directors: Andre Smagghe and Noel Howard
Screenplay: Robert Bolt (Michael Wilson, uncredited)
Cinematographer: F. A. Young (70mm Panavision; Technicolor)
Second Unit Photography: Skeets Kelly, Nicholas Roeg, Peter Newbrook
Special Effects: Cliff Richardson
Production Designer: John Box
Art Director: John Stoll
Set Decorator: Dario Simoni
Costumes: Phyllis Dalton
Music: Maurice Jarre
Sound: Paddy Cunningham
Sound Editor: Winston Ryder
Editor: Ann V. Coates
Cast: Peter O'Toole (T. E. Lawrence), Alec Guinness (Prince Feisal), Anthony Quinn (Auda Abu Tayi), Jack Hawkins (General Allenby), Omar Sharif (Sherif Ali), Jose Ferrer (Turkish Bey), Anthony Quayle (Colonel Brighton), Claude Rains (Mr. Dryden), Arthur Kennedy (Jackson Bentley), Donald Wolfit (General Murray), I. S. Johan (Gasim), Gamil Ratib (Majid), Michel Ray (Ferraji), Zia Mohyeddin (Tafas), John Dimech (Daud), Howard Marion Crawford (Medical Officer), Jack Gwillim (Club Secretary), Hugh Miller (RAMC Colonel)
Running time: 221 minutes (premier); 200 minutes (general release); 184 minutes (1972 re-release)
Premier: December 1962
16mm rental: Images

DOCTOR ZHIVAGO (Carlo Ponti–Metro-Goldwyn-Mayer, 1965)
Producer: Carlo Ponti
Executive Producer: Arvid L. Griffin
Assistant Directors: Roy Stevens, Pedro Vidal
Second Unit Director: Roy Rossotti
Screenplay: Robert Bolt, from the novel by Boris Pasternak
Photography: Freddie Young
Second Unit Photography: Manuel Berenguer
Special Effects: Eddie Fowlie

Production Designer: John Box
Art Director: Terence Marsh
Assistant Art Directors: Ernest Archer, Bill Hutchinson, Roy Walker
Set Decorator: Dario Simoni
Costumes: Phyllis Dalton
Music: Maurice Jarre
Sound: Paddy Cunningham
Sound Editor: Winston Ryder
Editor: Norman Savage
Cast: Omar Sharif (Yuri Zhivago), Julie Christie (Lara), Geraldine Chaplin (Tonya Gromeko Zhivago), Tom Courtenay (Pasha/Strelnikov), Alec Guinness (General Yevgref Zhivago), Siobhan McKenna (Anna Gromeko), Ralph Richardson (Alexander Gromeko), Rod Steiger (Komarovsky), Rita Tushingham (the girl, Tonya), Adrienne Corri (Lara's Mother), Geoffrey Keen (Professor Kurt), Jeffrey Rockland (Sasha Zhivago), Lucy Westmore (Katya), Noel William (Razin), Gerard Tichy (Liberius), Klaus Kinski (Kostoyed), Jack MacGowran (Petya), Maria Martin (Gentlewoman), Tarek Sharif (Yuri at age eight), Mercedes Ruiz (Tonya at age seven), Roger Maxwell (Colonel in charge of replacements), Inigo Jackson (Major), Virgilio Texeira (Captain), Bernard Kay (Bolshevik deserter), Erik Chitty (Old Soldier), Jose Nieto (the Priest), Mark Eden (Young Engineer)
Running time: 197 (193?) minutes (premier); 180 minutes (general release)
Premier: December 1965
16mm rental: Films, Inc.

RYAN'S DAUGHTER (Faraway Productions, A. G. Film/Metro-Goldwyn-Mayer, 1970)
Producer: Anthony Havelock-Allen
Associate Producer: Roy Stevens
Assistant Directors: Pedro Vidal, Michael Stevenson
Second Unit Directors: Roy Stevens (storm sequence), Charles Frend
Screenplay: Robert Bolt
Cinematographer: Freddie Young
Second Unit Photography: Denys Coop and Bob Huke
Special Effects: Robert MacDonald
Production Designer: Stephen Grimes
Art Director: Roy Walker
Set Decorator: Josie MacAvin
Costumes: Jocelyn Richards
Music: Maurice Jarre
Sound: John Bramall
Sound Editors: Ernie Grimsdale and Winston Ryder
Editor: Norman Savage
Cast: Sarah Miles (Rosy Ryan), Robert Mitchum (Charles Shaughnessy), Trevor Howard (Father Hugh Collins), Christopher Jones (Major Randolph Doryan), John Mills (Michael), Leo McKern (Tom Ryan), Barry Foster (Tim O'Leary), Arthur O'Sullivan (McCardle), Evin Crowley (Moureen), Marie

Keen (Mrs. McCardle), Barry Jackson (Corporal), Douglas Sheldon (Driver), Philip O'Flynn (Paddy), Gerald Sim (Captain), Des Keogh (Lanky Private), Niall Toibin (O'Keefe), Donald Neligan (Moureen's boyfriend), Brian O'Higgins (Constable O'Conner), Niall O'Brien (Bernard)

Running time: 206 (196?) minutes (Roadshow); 165 minutes (U.S. General Release)

Premier: December 1970

16mm rental: Films, Inc.

Index